Published by The Mary Foundation
PO Box 26101, Fairview Park, OH 44126
www.catholicity.com

The Conversion of Marianne Collins
aka Woman, My Confession

Library of Congress Control Number: 2017950868

ISBN-10: 0-9646316-7-0
ISBN-13: 978-0-9646316-7-0

PRINTING HISTORY:
August 2017

Printed in the United States of America

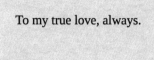
To my true love, always.

WOMAN

MY CONFESSION

—⚘

MARIANNE COLLINS

THE MARY FOUNDATION
Rocky River, Ohio

Acknowledgments

Many thanks to Paul and Carol Quist, Bud Macfarlane, and the Rev. John O'Brien, S.J., my dedicated editors.

Foreword

The names of Bear Woznick, Bert Mello, and some of Marianne's friends in the amazing story you are about to read are real. The names of others and certain details were changed to protect anonymity.

This autobiography was written for adults; parents are advised to use judgement before giving it to young-adult children.

After you finish, we respectfully request that you refrain from sharing the ending when you give this book to others.

Thank you.

Bud Macfarlane, Publisher
June 13, 2017
Feast of Saint Anthony

PART ONE

Passion

We must not be discouraged by our faults,
because children fall frequently.
Saint Thérèse of Lisieux

I believe in pink. I believe that laughing is the
best calorie burner. I believe in kissing, kissing a lot.
I believe that happy girls are the prettiest girls. I believe
tomorrow is another day and I believe in miracles.
Audrey Hepburn

My sacrifice, O God, is a contrite spirit.
A contrite, humbled heart, O God, you will not scorn.
Psalm 51: 18-19

Walk while you have the light, lest the darkness
overtake you. He who walks in the darkness
does not know where he goes.
Jesus of Nazareth

Where did you leave your baby?
Bleeding in her bed, her ghost has come to stay,
Oh you can try, you can't chase her away…
*Fastball, **Which Way to the Top?***

The Billy Pattern

I heard a sharp crack and pain shot into my head as his fist connected with my nose. I collapsed to the ground next to his little pick-up truck. It was so dark out—there were no streetlights where he had abruptly stopped near a railroad crossing before throwing my handbag out the window. Before this he had been screaming at me for several minutes while driving like a maniac. When I scrambled out to gather my things, which I could barely see, he followed me, still yelling, then grabbed me by the arms and began shaking me harshly. Then came the blow.

We were sixteen years old.

"Oh my God, O my God I'm so sorry!" he cried out, fumbling to lift me up, blood streaming down my chin.

I was in shock and did not know what to say or how to react. The person who had just struck me in the face was sincerely trying to help me recover from being hit in the face. Eventually he coaxed me back into his car. He kept apologizing all the way back to his house. We went to his bedroom and laid down on his bed. He was soothing; he told me how much he loved me, over and over, and how sorry he was.

I don't remember much more of what happened that night, but I do know I continued to go out with Billy for another two years, and this was the second to last time he hit me, but one of many dozens of times he verbally abused me.

With high hopes I had started that day, the Fourth of July, 1983. It ended with the numb, throbbing emotional pain coursing through my body, my heart, and my mind.

My relationship with Billy became the template for my relationships with men for the rest of my life.

On the night Billy hit me, I was a junior at a public high school in a nice suburban town. My parents loved each other in their own way. I was the youngest of six with two sisters and three brothers. I never attended Catholic schools, although my family went to Mass every Sunday. I do not remember anything substantial from the Catholic religious education classes (we called it "CCD") that public school children were required to attend.

I was introverted and shy, so I took in everything when we went to Mass. I was not fully aware Jesus was in the Eucharist; I believed I was watching a symbolic reenactment of the Last Supper. I did feel secure and comfortable in the routines of the liturgy. I clung to my mother's arm and placed my head on her shoulders— this was one of the only times during childhood when I received the physical affection I craved. Sometimes I daydreamed, like most children. I felt uplifted when Mass was over. I believed it inspired me to become Christlike and to treat others with kindness. However, especially as I entered my teenage years, I did not feel anything spiritual inside and did not understand the depth of the sacraments (on the night of my Confirmation I went to a sleepover at my girlfriend's house and we played the Ouija board).

After puberty I shed my bashfulness. I was known for having friends in every social group. Before I became involved with Billy, I was a straight-A student, a cheerleader, and sophomore class president. I was respected by students and teachers alike. I was kind to everyone.

When you were in high school, you knew girls like me. I was that girl.

Billy transferred to my school when we were both

juniors. He pursued me sweetly, walking me to every class. He was classically surfer boy handsome—like Rob Lowe. People called us "the Models." Our friends loved our mutual energy. I plugged him into my social circles. He plugged me into drugs and alcohol. Within weeks we began spending all of our free time together. We were infatuated to the point of obsession, especially him. He was insanely, irrationally jealous. He was also the class clown and people enjoyed having him around.

Within months I gradually lost track of my friends—a pattern I later found out was typical of an abusive-cycle relationship. I got high with Billy frequently, at times smoking marijuana almost every day. I was concerned about getting caught (and did not want to disappoint anyone in my family) but it never crossed my mind that taking drugs was wrong. I was living in the moment, enjoying my boyfriend.

Unfortunately, I had reasons to want to be away from my home life. My parent's relationship, despite a deep foundation of love, was dysfunctional—my mother was codependent, always making excuses for my father's sarcastic tongue, explosive temper, and difficult nature. My father, who had many good traits, was himself the son of a physically abusive father, and was emotionally immature—practically a child. During my years with Billy, my mother was also pouring herself into taking care of my father's mother who was dying slowly in our home. In addition to all this, my middle brother had cancer. It was horrible—I remember him coming home from chemotherapy and retching for hours. The sound and the smell were deeply disturbing.

No one was talking to me, consoling me, or explaining what was going on—it was simply not possible in my family for anyone to pay any attention to what would now be considered my childhood trauma. I had to figure out everything for myself. No prepubescent child would have had the wisdom or experience to comprehend the severity of my situation. In a certain real sense, I was left to raise myself.

School became my therapy. As long as I did well there, my parents left me to my own devices. I was social and I loved the structure. It gave me what I needed to feed my mind and I was with friends I had known since I was a little girl. Billy became my ultimate escape. When I was with him, he took me away from the overwhelmingly sad, emotionally draining reality of my home life.

I enjoyed smoking weed, especially when I was with Billy and our friends, who were, by-and-large, good students from respectable families.

Suburbia, 1980s.

I began skipping classes and neglecting my studies. I almost did not graduate from high school because my history class was after lunch—and lunch was when Billy often lost his temper. He screamed at me, threw me against a wall, tossed my gym clothes into the quad. I was so upset I often missed history class. Nobody knew what was going on—I was humiliated and did not want to spoil our facade of the ideal high school romance. Obviously, Billy did not want anyone to know how messed up he was.

Billy did not graduate with me. Because of his charming nature, exceptions were made so he was given ample opportunities to recover scholastically yet he continuously sabotaged his own success. He blamed me, not that he had a reason. He blamed me for anything that did not go well in his life rather than taking responsibility for his own actions. Most alcoholics are this way. (This is called *projection*—a textbook case for all you psychology majors.)

During my senior year I became fully intimate with

Billy (just before my seventeenth birthday). It was a mutual decision, not the result of his lobbying. We cared for each other and our bodies were taking over. There was no one to tell us it was wrong or why it was wrong.

I discussed this with my friend Jayne because she was sleeping with her boyfriend. I had already slept with Billy without protection. On the day our classmates voted for "Senior Bests," we cut school so Jayne could take me to a nearby Planned Parenthood. They just handed the pill to me. No cost. No forms. No counseling.

Soon after I discovered that I had been voted "Best Looking" in the senior class that day. I was surprised as I felt there were several beautiful young women in my peer group. What was it that set me apart? My classmates and I had been together since elementary school. Perhaps they recognized my stylishness, my charisma, and kindness? Looking back, I hope the combination of these qualities was shining through.

Now on the pill, Billy and I slept together much more often. I loved him; I felt no guilt. We were definitely going to get married. He was set to join the military. There was no doubt in my mind I wanted to have a family with him—and not in some vague future, but soon after high school. When he wasn't hurting me, he was charming, fun, hilarious, and quick-minded. Intimately, he was sensitive, emotional (more than I was), and tender. Even looking back after all these years, I am sure that he loved me too, at least as best he could in his immature way.

Oh, and he cheated on me by taking other girls out on a regular basis. He had a wandering eye and was a flirt—he was insecure and craved the limelight. Yet he became very agitated whenever I received any kind of attention. One time, when my high school had a "spirit week" I dressed up as my alter ego in an amazing punk outfit. Everyone loved it! I was ecstatic. Billy's outfit was dull, and when he saw that my get-up was a hit, he started yelling at me and stormed out of school early.

When I confronted him about cheating on me, sometimes he lied to cover it up, sometimes not. I justified his poor behavior for him, with him. I remember him telling me how sorry he was for cheating on me and I actually consoled him, saying, "I understand why you did what you did." I thought I was loving him by helping him overcome his guilt. (Textbook *codependency.*)

I stayed with him when he screamed at me. I stayed with him when he cheated on me. I stayed with him when he hit me. I held on to the tender version of him I knew from the beginning. I did not want to lose him, especially because we were planning to marry. So Fourth of July in 1983 was not particularly unusual. Earlier that day I was looking forward to going out with Billy to celebrate the holiday with friends. I remember the outfit I selected in anticipation of pleasing him: a cute white sun dress with a ruffled hem and a pink sash.

When he came by to pick me up, he looked me up and down as I twirled around, smiling and laughing. I saw his frown. "Don't you like my outfit?" I asked, my voice rising sweetly.

"Why would you wear something like that?" he replied in an acid tone. "Are you trying to get attention? You look like a slut."

Stung, I defended myself and we began arguing bitterly. I pulled his little gold promise ring from my finger and threw it at him. He left in a huff to go waterskiing and get drunk with his friends. I did not realize he was probably instigating a fight so he could leave me to do what he really wanted.

I trudged home, angry and hurt, aching inside, and listened to music. A neighbor came over and cajoled me into attending a party at the home of a boy named Rich

who I had dated several times. Billy knew that he was
a decent guy and was extremely jealous of him.

I was enjoying myself with Rich at the party when
one of Billy's friends approached me. He carefully
convinced me to go outside to "just say hello" to Billy,
who was waiting for me inside his new Datsun pick-up.
I climbed in reluctantly, and after a little bit of driving
around, from one second to the next he started berating
me and driving like a madman. He stopped at the dark
railroad crossing and you know what happened next.

—◄(◎

I am not trying to demonize Billy, as horrible as his
behavior was, and this autobiography is not a tell-all
or rant about all the men who hurt me. In fact, I will
leave out most of the details. He was immature and did
not know how to process his emotions. He was already
a heavy drinker. He himself was conceived through
an adulterous affair. His biological father never came
around and his stepfather was hard on his stepson for
being a poor student. Billy was as much a product of
our toxic culture as I was.

Billy believed completely in Jesus; he attended a non-
denominational Protestant Church. We once attended
church camp together. His parents were not pleased I
was a Catholic, but they loved me. My parents did not
like that he was not one, but Billy charmed them. They
did not know he was abusing me, getting drunk and high
with me, or sleeping with me.

Even though my mother's codependence manifested
in a different way, I was following in her footsteps.
My relationship with Billy caused a kind of inchoate
cognitive dissonance because I am, by temperament,
independent-minded. It is the oddest thing (and I have

heard this from my female friends who have experienced the same dynamic), but I would transform into my mother when I entered a romantic relationship. This happened without regard to how maturely and confidently I carried myself in professional or other settings. It is difficult to put into words, but I "shrunk" when I was with Billy. For example, I would consciously dim my vivaciousness at social events to make sure to avoid his wrath.

Our cycle repeated frequently. He instigated intense arguments, yelled at me, would leave and then come back to beg for forgiveness, and I would forgive him; then we would share some tender moments, and then it would happen again, then again. Every week or so. Dozens of times a year. Billy was always talking about "creating a clean slate." To this day I cannot stand that phrase.

I also recall the adrenaline rush when we were fighting. It was a dark, addictive drug. It got to a point that normal—that is, when we were not fighting—was abnormal, and it was difficult to live with the calm.

Discord was calm. Calm was discord.

And because I truly loved him, however immaturely, instead of considering ending the relationship, I kept trying to repair it. A common thrust of Billy's arguing was to accuse me of causing the problem even though he was always the instigator. I began to wonder if he was correct. I became confused.

Confusion is a part of the cycle. All these irrational thoughts are taking up residence in your mind, drummed in by powerful emotions—anger, shock, sorrow, elation, sexual ecstasy. They sink deep roots into your psyche. The drugs we were taking did not help. A certainty that abuse is normal in a relationship takes hold inside you. It becomes neurological: your very thoughts begin to betray you. This is quite disorienting. You become accustomed to the pattern, the repetitiveness. Some of my readers know exactly what I am writing about since you have lived through a similar cycle—as the abuser or the abused.

Part of the aftermath is the theft of the spirit of who you really are, of who Christ made you to be. Out of fear of a blow-up I found myself permanently walking on eggshells. I spent tremendous amounts of psychic energy self-editing everything I did and said when I was with Billy. When he was not around, I was constantly in planning mode, trying to anticipate how to avoid trouble. You strategize mentally for hours, habitually, when you are not with the abuser. It is as if you are at war and the enemy is your best friend.

Imagine this is your state of mind, day after day, month after month.

Under this kind of pressure and fear you simply cannot be yourself around the person you believe you love. Even if you are "perfect," any pretense can be used to trigger the mistreatment, but you don't know this. You don't know that you will be hurt again no matter what you do, no matter how well you plan to avoid it.

For the sake of my readers, perhaps especially if you have not been abused in this way, it is important to understand how deeply the cycle of brutality cuts into your soul. Of course the intensity of the immediate emotional pain is searing. The trauma of being screamed at and called the foulest of names is both shocking and surreal. It simply does not make any sense that this person you love is treating you so hatefully.

Why is this happening? Minutes and hours and days later the heartache is still intense. It stays with you. You are not "okay" in class or at work the next day.

Yet the long term aftermath is even worse, potentially leading to decades of suffering. This can foster despair. In this sense the psychological abuse far exceeds the physical abuse. Without grace and healing, future relationships and choices are likely pre-poisoned by subconscious mental habits you do not realize exist. My nose recovered from the blow, but nearly four decades later I am still dealing with the repercussions of the psychological damage.

I know some people might read that last line and be tempted to advise me or others, "Stop being so fragile—you had a bad boyfriend in high school, so move on and get over it." If this is what you believe, you should thank God, because you likely have never experienced the soul-numbing reality of the abuse cycle—or you are simply misinformed. Many millions of children, women and men are abused daily in our post-modern society. The scars are real. For so many, the wounds are still bleeding, and healing has not taken place or is incomplete. Chances are, someone (and more likely multiple people) close to you—a sister, a friend, a coworker, a neighbor, or a parent—is suffering from long-term pain and harmful choices that result from the cycle, perhaps decades after the fact.

Where were my parents and siblings in all this? My parents did not know what I was experiencing and I never considered sharing any of this with them. Besides, we were not close in the way I wanted to be close. My mother loved me but she did not express this verbally until I was thirty-five years old—and even then, I had to lobby her to do so. My father has never told me he loves me, although he tried to show me with actions such as building ornate dollhouses for me when I was a child. If I had disclosed what was happening with Billy, they would have told me to stop dating him immediately.

There was no way I was going to stop being with the boy I loved and longed to marry someday.

Nor was I going to tell my brothers. I was not close to them. One of my older sisters had eloped and moved away when I was fourteen. My other sister was three years older and busy with her own life and problems. She was from the same dysfunctional family, after all.

As for my female friends, I grew weary of telling the few I trusted about Billy's behavior. Just telling them was humiliating. I found myself distancing myself from my closer friends, then eventually losing them. This isolation effect is common. Besides, most thought Billy was wonderful and sincerely felt the status and benefits of having such "a catch" was worth putting up with his occasional difficulties. Like me, they minimized his responsibility. As a result, ironically, the one who hurt me became my closest friend, and in some ways, my only true friend. I was worse off than ever.

After high school Billy joined the Army and moved away. He sent touching, loving letters, mostly focused on our future life together. I remained faithful to him. Somehow he was released early and returned a year later with a tattoo on his arm featuring a rose above my nickname.

But the pattern of abuse-forgiveness-abuse continued. One time he jumped on my car as I drove away from a vicious argument and broke the windshield with his fist. I told my mother a pheasant caused the damage. A *pheasant!*

Without direction in his life at the time, Billy was depressed and treated me kindly less often. Our high hopes seemed to dissipate like a fog. Within a year I finally broke up with him semi-permanently and began dating other men.

I left home after high school when I was seventeen with no financial support or educational guidance from my parents. I was on my own, alone. I was nineteen when I broke up with Billy and was attending night school at a junior college while working nearly full-time at a large technology conglomerate. I eventually began seeing a nice man—remember Rich from high school? Although he was a fallen away Catholic, he was decent, sweet, and respectful in terms of sexuality. Unfortunately, he lived in another state and it just did not work out.

After Rich I dated a man I met at work. Pete was an East Coast guy, so he had a dry sense of humor and was very loyal. A child of divorce, he was raised Catholic but fell away because his mother stopped practicing. He was a good man, intelligent, but his work was more important to him than I was. I was on the pill and slept with him regularly without any guilt. It made me feel closer to him (because that is what sex is designed to do); I believed very sincerely that we would be married one day. We both wanted to have children.

Even so, I broke up with him because he was a workaholic; we had stopped doing things together as often. I lost interest. I stopped believing he loved me because I was second fiddle to his career. We drifted apart but kept on good terms—he has remained a loyal friend to this day.

Neither of these two boyfriends were abusive, so the psychological patterns engraved into my heart when I was teenager had not been addressed and were not apparent to me. I was still in touch with Billy, and in fact, he called me at least once a year to find out how I was doing. He lived nearby and our relationship transformed into a platonic friendship.

As far as my faith was concerned, I gradually began attending Mass less often, especially after I moved out. During these years, I went sporadically, although I considered myself a respectful Catholic. I had not been to Confession since grammar school—I did not even know I should have been going several times a year. Like most of my friends and most people from my poorly-catechized generation, I knew very little about the Catholic faith. We were criminally neglected in this respect. (Until last year I was not aware the *Catechism of the Catholic Church* existed.)

There are a lot of evangelical Protestants in my part of the country and they told me I didn't need to go to Confession and that Catholic practices were man-made.

Despite my sporadic practice of the faith, I always loved Mary, the Mother of God. I knew she was special. I did not realize there were devotions to her. I knew there was a Rosary, but I had not prayed it as a child. Ironically, my parents prayed the Rosary every night but did not teach it to us. Every once in a blue moon, they had us pray it with them, but all I knew was the Our Father and Hail Mary—I knew nothing about the Mysteries designed for meditation based upon the key events in the lives of Jesus and Mary.

Even so, if someone had asked me what I thought about God, I would have said without hesitation, calmly, and with conviction, "I completely believe in God." I had the *gift of faith* yet I did not have a *life of faith*. Praying was not a regular part of my daily life. Being consciously grateful to God for my talents, blessings, for the good people who loved me—this was a foreign concept to me. I was enjoying spending time with my boyfriend on weekends, traveling, going to college, working, and making my own way in life.

It also brought me joy to help people and to be a light

in the lives of others; I was eager to do this every day with the people at work. Looking back, I did not realize what I was missing in terms of my faith. The gift I was given at baptism, faith, was like a barely discernible ember, authentic but dormant. Maybe you are this way right now. Although I was having difficulty understanding the depth of the sacraments, when I did attend Mass, I always knew it was a safe place for me to be. It was a sanctuary. In a life filled with turbulence, it remained a haven of peace.

Blinking Red Light

I met my first "husband" on a blind date when I was twenty-one years old. Let's call him Tom. The same girl who took me to Planned Parenthood years before set me up on the date. I should have known.

He was engaging, humorous, artistic, and full of energy. We dated for three years before we got married. I was working for a large insurance company in claim litigation. Although I was still on the pill, we planned to have children someday.

We lived an adventurous lifestyle and enjoyed a large social circle of like-minded friends. Travelled to island paradises all over North America. Enjoyed our food; he was a fine chef. Made our own beer before it was all the rage. Many of our activities involved scuba diving and free diving. We bought a house together and entertained friends at dinner parties. He was a talented musician and wrote songs for me.

We rarely went to Mass. Our Sundays consisted of listening to smooth jazz, reading the paper, enjoying a cup of coffee, and recapping our week at work. I did not feel guilty about missing Mass—that I was breaking the commandment to keep the Lord's Day holy never crossed my mind. I did not know it was a commandment. Because Tom would always put up a fuss about going with me, I attended the big ones alone—Easter and Christmas.

I wanted to get married in the Catholic Church; this was non-negotiable for me. Tom did not practice any kind of faith, although his mother was a deeply committed Christian. He agreed to be married in the Catholic

Church but did not convert. When the priest in charge of our marriage preparation asked him about his faith, Tom confirmed that he believed in God, and Father responded, "Well, that's good enough for me."

Tom promised to go Mass with me and to raise our children Catholic. About six months before we separated, he told me that he did not want to have children, as well.

He lost his temper over small matters. I never knew when it would happen. I do not recall him apologizing over the course of the seven years I knew him.

On the positive side he was generous and a reliable provider. Somewhat typically, as the son of an alcoholic, he was oriented toward pleasing others. He never cared about being thanked. And when he was good to me, he was really good—kind, fun, interesting, and a joy to be around.

My reaction to the mistreatment was to close in upon myself—withdraw. I did not respond to him during his outbursts. I was in shock. It was an eerily similar cycle to what had happened with Billy in high school, but unlike Billy, he was not apologetic, and this time I was married.

After a conflict, he would say nothing for a while, then try to make up for it by cooking something he knew I liked. Nothing was ever resolved—our problems were swept under the rug without any communication, forgiveness, or honesty. This happened several times a year, year after year. He did not want to go to counseling. After every incident I grew more numb inside. I never considered leaving him because I was committed to my vows. I took "for better or for worse" seriously. I know some of you can relate.

I accepted his flaws as a part of who he was. Even so, I was consciously aware before I got married *that I should not have married him.* I had a nagging inkling that we should have remained friends. Some of this cognitive dissonance (that is: living, believing, or acting according to contradictory ideas) was a psycho-physiological effect of my being on the pill, which I will explain in a little bit.

Additionally, I was not particularly attracted to his looks. We had little physical chemistry. Rather, I was taken in by his charming personality and energy. Before the wedding I had a strange dream wherein I was prevented from becoming a nun and teaching children because of the impending marriage—I took it as a sign to reconsider, then ignored it along with my other conscious reservations. The momentum of years of dating and years of living together slowly propelled me forward into a pseudo-marriage. Is this your story, too?

Toward the end, he became emotionally distant and ceased engaging in deep conversations. Unannounced, he left with the guys for weekends on adventures out of state. He "messed with my head" with baseless criticism and strange, out-of-left-field mind games. We stopped having relations and he rarely touched me during this time. We were cordial with each other and he still cooked for me. We were more roommates than husband and wife. Over this stretch, the energy seeped out of me, and my normal bright light from my teenage years and early twenties grew dim.

—◄◖

Please remember that I was in my late twenties. Sexual activity had been demystified, was guilt-free, and was more or less separated from the thought of procreation. Nowadays, for teenagers who have been exposed to pornography since before latency, oral sex on the first date is often considered on the same level as a good-night kiss for prior generations.

By the time I was dating Tom, it had become possible for sex to become a kind of physical comfort food. Looking back, it is striking that I was not particularly attracted to him for his looks. I was drawn to his charisma, but this had not translated into strong sexual chemistry. It might be difficult for a devout Catholic reader to understand that whether a non-Christian or poorly-formed Christian begins sleeping with a boyfriend or girlfriend on the first day or third week, even the most advanced sexual activity can have the same emotional impact as kissing. The secular world is the sex-ular world.

Sexual activity, in a "committed relationship" or for physical pleasure, can be little different from enjoying a glass of wine. Some wine is wonderful. Some less so. This is the inevitable result of a society which separates sexuality from morality. Objectively, sexual activity is fun and filled with pleasure. If you believe you love the other person or feel a connection, it provides even more psychic pleasure (or comfort). Under these circumstances, ask yourself: why would any teenager or young man or woman deny themselves?

That was my world.

Young women today, even younger than I was in high school, believe that they must give their bodies to attract and keep a boy. These are usually the young women whose fathers are absent, abusive, emotionally distant (and never hear "I love you" from their fathers, which was the case with me), or do not have a strong faith. If a girl does not feel safe and secure in her father's love or the love of Jesus, the first lust-motivated boy to come along and convince her she is beautiful and wonderful has a very high likelihood of having advanced sexual activity with her.

I will share more about the pill later in this book, but I have to add at this juncture that I believe these power-ful artificial hormones that we women blithely put into our bodies have known psychological effects that were detrimental to my relationship and decision-making with Tom. At the time, I was not aware of these effects. I have recently learned that the hormones in the pill cross up or suppress the natural psycho-physiological signals between men and women. In my case (and you can probably relate if you have ever used the pill) taking the pill contributed strongly to my mistakenly believing that we were compatible when we were not. In other words, without the pill reducing and distorting my libido and sexual desires, I would have realized how obvious it was that Tom and I were not sexually attracted or "matched." Had I not been on the pill, I sincerely doubt I would have considered him as a "mate" for marriage and probably would have simply remained friends.

Not too many years after Billy, now several years into my relationship with Tom, this stale sexual ethos had transformed me into a roommate with my own husband. I did not understand why he had become so cold. The years of alienation had suppressed any desire to have him touch me. I eventually suggested that we should consider taking some time apart. A few weeks later he asked for a separation without discussing divorce.

For the next few weeks I slowly packed my things. He slept in the same bed with me every night, includ-ing the last night before I moved. He consoled me. The next morning he helped me take everything to my new place.

A week or so later, while he was on vacation, using an extra set of keys he did not know about, I let myself into our house and the shock began to build slowly. A new set of coffee mugs. Slightly different décor. In Tom's handwriting, a woman's name jotted on the calendar.

The answering machine was in the bedroom; the red light was blinking. On the nightstand was a card with the following message: "Looking forward to a nauseatingly perfect relationship with you. XOXO," signed with the same name as the one on the calendar. The deep, cutting sense of betrayal and humiliation was so palpable it took over my body. It was gut-wrenching.

At this point I could not *not* press the answering machine button. I heard the matronly voice of an older woman. When I called to ask how she knew Tom, she answered enthusiastically, in a high-pitched voice, "Oh, that's my daughter's boyfriend!"

"Well my name is Marianne," I informed her calmly. "And I am his wife."

I obtained the civil divorce as quickly as possible and walked away without financial benefit. I did not want to endure one more minute of association with this man.

—◀◎

I was twenty-nine years old, had a solid career and was free. I went to Mass hoping it would make me feel better, but it didn't help. I tried to be stoic. To numb the pain, I threw myself into my job and finishing my degree—I had no life outside of work and school.

I was well established as the black sheep of the family by this point. My mother, at some level, had known that something was off with the marriage, and supported me, but neither one of my parents could relate to my situation. I barely understood it myself.

I had tried to be a loving wife and companion. I was faithful. Yet looking back now, over two decades later, I truly was unaware of what the sacrament of marriage could be.

A year after the civil divorce, the Catholic Church determined that our union was invalid. As the expression goes, I received an annulment. I went through the entire process and found it cathartic—answering the questions with honesty, discerning my faulty decision-making, presenting witnesses, and accepting my own shortcomings and errors in judgement. I sought the annulment because I wanted to clear my conscience. I recognized that our civil marriage was not what God's definition of *sacramental* marriage is.

Not long after, at a class reunion, Billy approached me and asked to speak in private. Still handsome, some of his old charisma had faded as he stood before me in a hallway, away from the noise. He explained how he had cleaned up his act and was going through the Twelve Steps in the Alcoholics Anonymous program. Then he sincerely apologized for hurting me during high school and afterwards. He did not make excuses and seemed genuinely sorry.

I accepted his apology and wished him well. I was happy for him. He had married and had started a family. Although at the time his apology did not make me feel better—I was still emotionally numb from the divorce—to this day Billy is the only one who has ever apologized to me. We still keep in touch and share mutual friends in my hometown. He is a good man who was able to break the cycle. His story, like mine, is one of redemption.

I would like to take some time to share with you something that has plagued me my whole life, perfectionism, and how this influenced what became decades of harmful relationships with men. The seeds of perfectionism took root during early childhood. In grammar school I took great pride in solving math problems, but if I came across an equation I did not know how to solve, it paralyzed me. I would sit at my desk while the other students would be excused for recess, staring down at my sheet, the clock on the wall tick-ticking by, until salty water welled in my eyes, growing into larger drops that fell onto the worksheet. My tears spread on the sheet and diluted the ink that formed the lines on the cheap paper. Deep anguish.

Asking for help was painful and paralyzing. I would approach a teacher and literally not be able to speak any words. I could not find my voice. Asking for help represented a kind of failure not dissimilar to failing to complete the assignment correctly—perfectly.

As I grew older the perfectionism understandably manifested as excellent work in grammar school, so it was reinforced by teachers and my parents. Being "perfect" became part of my self-identity. During my teenage years, I became more social, and you already know about Billy. The perfectionist in me could not allow anyone (especially my family members and my high school friends) to know the secret defects of that relationship.

Perfectionism is about masks—masking failure, masking insecurity. You perfectionists understand. My mask was to appear happy—to seem as though I had it all together. People expected me to be buoyant and to meet their high expectations. I never let anyone know about my interior pain and confusion. Sometimes I built the facade so well that there were times I believed it myself—until the next Billy or Tom came along.

In the professional world, perfectionism manifests in

becoming performance driven. This happened to me. If you have any talent at all, the result of perfectionism is usually excellent results. Good results are, understandably, rewarded in our business culture. In this way perfectionism becomes a self-reinforcing cycle.

All these years later, it is interesting that I could not find my voice to defend myself during these damaging relationships. However, I was able to find the words to help other people in my life, including the men who hurt me, coworkers, friends, and the many people who came into my life through volunteer work.

———◀◉

I began seeing an introverted man named Stan. We met because we lived in the same large home with another person as housemates. When I moved out to my own condominium, Stan gradually contacted me less often. I looked in the mirror one Saturday morning and sincerely asked God for help. "You know, God, I'm not sure what's going on. Good, bad or indifferent, if you could just show me what is happening with Stan, I would appreciate it."

Within a matter of days, through a series of relatively banal "coincidences," I discovered that he had been cheating on me with another woman. It hurt, yet God had answered my prayer. I initially liked Stan because he seemed to be the opposite of the others, but he turned out to be a self-centered cad.

My next relationship, sadly, followed a variation of the pattern. For two years I dated a very handsome man named Elliot, who was a financial savant. Although he had millions in the bank, he was an extraordinary skinflint (to save a few dollars he loaded his suitcases with canned food when we went on our only vacation).

Although sweet in the beginning, he began verbally abusing me sporadically—explosive bursts with the foulest language, including once in public. Ultimately, he turned out to be an emotionally stunted, passive-aggressive narcissist. On some level, maybe that is why I chose him. I don't know.

I slept with him but the relationship was more based on companionship than sensuality. He assured me I was beautiful, yet pressured me to have breast augmentation. I cut my hair short to please him despite a lifetime of being known for my trademark voluminous mane.

We never lived together. We went to Mass on Easter and Christmas and a few other times, but neither of us understood the faith. We did not pray together or talk about God. Our life was about doing things together—very worldly.

Elliot did not cheat on me. He told me he wanted to have a baby and we shopped frequently for expensive homes in anticipation of marriage. I did everything I could to be the perfect companion, although he was loathe to express gratitude.

After one of his outbursts, I left him. At that point I was no longer emotionally invested, so I felt free. Two years wasted on a shell of a man like so many men in modern society. I rarely thought about him until writing this autobiography. Like others before him, he wanted the light that shone out of me, but yet when he had me, he suppressed it.

—◄◖

Still, I always had high hopes to find happiness through marriage. In retrospect I never asked God for a good Catholic man—I did not know that I could. Given my superficial practice of the faith, I admit I did not know

what a good Catholic man would be like. I believed
that meeting a good man was a matter of being at the
right place at the right time and that it would eventually
happen to me.

During this time I also began delving into occult
philosophies such as astrology and numerology. I was
ignorant of the dangers; I was sincerely interested
in finding the truth about life and its meaning. I was
searching for tools for my spiritual "toolbox." Rather
than spending time learning about my Catholic faith, I
was spending time reading book after book containing
these ultimately misleading and corrosive ideas. I met
for sessions with a spiritual "healer" who was heavily
reliant upon questionable practices. I read the same
spiritually dangerous books that millions of people
from our generation read. The ideas I adopted led to
bad decisions.

Nothing—absolutely nothing—in my Catholic education or upbringing contained the slightest warning
about the grave risks of the occult or misleading (even
if genuinely sincere) non-Christian and non-Catholic
spiritual "experts." I still believed in Jesus but obviously did not feel His presence or I might have taken a
different path.

After breaking up with Elliot I attended Mass alone,
infrequently. Like the vast majority of Catholics today,
I received Communion despite not having gone to
Confession since childhood. I didn't know what sacri-
legious reception of Communion was, that not having
a conversation with Jesus every day (praying) was a
contradiction for a Christian, that sleeping with the men
I cared about was wrong, or that missing Mass was a
serious sin. None of these things were discussed in my
family. I had no mentor. No one, neither my older sisters
nor my parents, told me that sex before marriage was

wrong (in fact, we did not talk about sex or sexuality at all). Nothing.

In romantic relationships I was alone, adrift, receiving questionable advice from girlfriends who were just as clueless as I was. As just one example, the mother of one of my closest friends from grammar school put her daughter on the pill at age fourteen. This was the morality-neutral, religiously vapid atmosphere that engulfed me.

Death Spiral

I worked long hours to fill my interior emptiness and the void in my evenings of not having a mate. I started attending Mass at the city cathedral, drawn to a liberal priest there. Even though I believed in God and considered myself a good Catholic, I was arrogant. During Mass at that time in my life, just before Communion was distributed, I refused to pray the following prayer out loud with the rest of the congregation: "Lord I am not worthy to receive you, but only say the word and my soul shall be healed."

I am not saying that, I told myself. I considered myself worthy, partly due to my pride, partly due to my ignorance, and in large part because of my lack of understanding of what the Eucharist truly is—the real presence of Christ—body, blood, soul, and divinity.

I eventually started dating a good man I met in the office. Brad initiated the relationship. He had grown up in the Midwest and was seven years younger. We dated for a year and he eventually asked me to marry him on a giant balloon ride at an air show. My immediate reaction was that I simply could not say yes. This was embarrassing for Brad, but I had not recovered from the divorce and two toxic years with Elliot. In retrospect I believe I needed to fill the space in my heart with Jesus, not another man.

Unfortunately, seeing how upset Brad was, I quickly asked him to ask me again, and then I said yes. He was thrilled but I had my reservations. He enthusiastically signed up for RCIA and I was his sponsor to enter the Catholic Church. He was quite diligent; this disturbed his deeply anti-Catholic mother, which I took as a sign that he must have been serious.

Yet the minute we became engaged I transformed into a critical and disrespectful person—contrary to my typical disposition. You know the word that is used to describe this kind of woman. It begins with the letter *b*. That's what I was to Brad. I did not realize at the time that I was sabotaging the relationship.

We had the church, the dress, the reception hall. About three months before the wedding, we broke up. It was a mutual decision, given my disrespectful treatment of him. I had been pushing him away since he gave me the ring. I felt guilty for helping Brad become a Catholic but not helping him *be a Catholic*.

I was in such a dark spirit that I lost fifteen pounds; because I have never been overweight this was very unhealthy. There was a demonic quality to my guilt. I would look at food and say to myself, "I have hurt Brad so deeply that I don't deserve to eat." I was living on less than two hundred calories a day.

—◀◉

In the weeks and months after the break-up I began spending social time with two different sets of friends. One group consisted of relatively wholesome, successful people who were a positive influence even though they were not particularly Christian.

The other group I called the "night crawlers." With this set of friends, the main activity consisted of meeting at a particular restaurant to drink, play pool, eat good food, and listen to music.

It was here that I met a man who I shall not name. He was a retired professional athlete with an air of confidence. He liked to show off his two Super Bowl rings. He had been divorced multiple times.

We lived the high life—the best of everything: restaurants, cars, hotels, and front row seats at every stadium, concert, or arena. He was an alcoholic. We were not committed to each other so I was not sleeping with him at the time.

I made poor decisions when I was with him. On Good Friday in 2003, I had a choice between having a wholesome fish dinner with the good group of friends or going out drinking with this man. I went out with him and we got drunk that night and again on Holy Saturday. I was so hung over that I missed Mass on Easter Sunday. On some level I knew he was a bad influence—another verbally abusive alcoholic. Feeling truly guilty over the Easter debacle, I stopped seeing him.

Satan was after me. A few months later, amidst a dark fog of loneliness, I called the man on Father's Day after feeling this strange pull. We decided to see each other that afternoon. I was not on the pill and that evening after having too much to drink I slept with him. Within days I left with some friends on a vacation in Europe. During the weeks there I remember being so ill that I did not socialize at all; I chalked it up to the rigors of traveling.

When I returned home I discovered I was pregnant. My revulsion at having a child who would be connected to this dark-souled man was instantaneous and become my rationale for deciding to get an abortion. I could not think straight. I was angry, absolutely livid. I could not entertain the thought of anything else. I could not allow myself to think of it as a pregnancy. Although I had always been the classic pro-life girl during discussions in college, I could not contemplate any alternative. When I told the father, he eagerly made all the arrangements and brought me to a well-respected physician.

He paid this doctor $800 in cash.

The doctor gave me two chances before the procedure. He asked me if I wanted to hear the heartbeat. He offered to show me the ultrasound. He did this not to help me, but to help himself sleep at night by minimizing his choice to do what he did. (He told me afterwards, casually if not coldly, "I bring babies into the world and I take babies out of the world and it's all the same to me.")

When it was over, as I lay there, I felt something on me, on the inside of my leg. A trickle of blood. A huge tear formed in my right eye and streamed down my cheek.

It was July 26th, forty days after Father's Day.

From that moment forward, I refused to let myself think about it…until July 26th comes around, when I cannot help it. There have been fifteen July 26ths.

I will say this, with tears streaming down my face as I type, that every man who has ever abused me played their role in taking me to that office and participated in the death spiral of what happened on that horrible day.

—◦)⊙

In the aftermath, I descended deeper into a mental abyss. I was working insane hours. I was still seeing this man, still under his spell; he convinced me to form a joint investment account. I discovered weeks later that he was secretly withdrawing money from it—he had taken advantage of my emotional confusion and vulnerability as an opportunity to run a financial scam.

I ended the relationship when I found out.

I was drawn toward an even darker place. He had been the ultimate emotional vampire. I completely repressed what we had done. I did not pray about it or bring it to God. It was as if it had never happened.

Soon after, from my circle of "good friends," I met a relatively more normal man with a nice personality. He even attended Mass with me. Even though I was on the pill, for the first time I became paranoid about becoming pregnant and regularly took pregnancy tests. I was so screwed up that I did not comprehend the connection to losing my child. I broke up with him and dated other creeps. From my group of "night crawlers," I became involved with a mentally unstable stalker with a malignant spirit.

My judgment, discernment, and intuition about men were now seriously impaired, but I was not aware of it.

I was doing very well at the insurance company, but my responsibilities made me the target of a certain amount of verbal abuse, sometimes severe, from dissatisfied clients. This added to my stress. I became so out of sorts that I began seeing a therapist. I did not tell her about what had happened with the dark-souled man. But I began to lose my will to live and one day I frankly told her, "I wish I was not here."

She immediately had me institutionalized without my consent for three days. This was a nightmare—the disorientation, the drugs, being manhandled, the loss of control over my own life. I could actually feel and see the evil all around me, appearing as a greyish fog. When the three days were over, I could not leave fast enough.

After I was released, even though I took sick days off from work, I did not feel whole—it was as if I were split into two different people: an insane woman and a "working" version of myself at the same time. I was also suffering from the effects of a concussion when a brute, goofing around, accidentally dropped me on my head at a party.

When I returned to work, for the first time in my career I started performing poorly. I lost my ability to focus and eventually resigned.

—◀(◎

I was introduced to Luke through my group of good friends in fall of 2004. He was a widower with a teen-age daughter and a successful corporate executive. We became serious and began to plan a life together. He did not mistreat me, and even if a bit dull, was reliable and sweet. We were formally engaged within six months and I spent many nights at his home—I practically lived there, and became close to his daughter.

Before we were engaged he willingly entered RCIA to convert to Catholicism; he asked me to be his sponsor. We were planning to move to Singapore via a company promotion and together we picked out the names for the two children we decided to have. Luke entered the Catholic church on Easter 2005 and we went to church on Sunday together. We held hands during Mass.

Finally.

Finally I was, for certain, going to be married to a decent man, a Catholic man, and have a family! I was thirty-seven years old, free from my soul-sucking job at the insurance company (where I had labored for fourteen years). I was finally, finally happy and on the right track.

We very carefully mapped out my "official" move to his home. On the day of the move, with half of my belongings already in his house and the other half in the moving truck, his daughter called to give Luke an ultimatum. She played on his grief over her deceased mother. It was me or her.

He caved. He meekly informed me that I could not move in. We were finished. No longer able to stay in my

own condo, I had no place to live. I landed in a hotel.
My pending marriage to Luke ended after one phone
call from a spoiled sixteen-year-old.

—◄◎

In some ways, the break-up was a blessing in disguise.
I received an unexpected, modest financial windfall
through a class action suit, so I took the summer off.
Remember, I had been on my own since I was seventeen,
put myself through college, and had been working crazy
hours for two decades. It was my first break without any
responsibility since childhood. No pet. No boyfriend.
No job. No pressing need for money.

I was free.

I needed to heal, although I was not aware of it.

I spent that summer living in luxury hotels. I spoiled
myself. Although Coco Chanel black has always been
my favorite fashion color, I made a conscious decision
to not wear a stitch of black all summer. I wanted everything to be bright, white, and optimistic. I read books. I
was also able to walk into a social engagement and walk
out with a man—I had no interest in dating seriously
and exchanged one for another three times that summer.

I began reading books by Marianne Williamson, a
Jewish Christian spiritual writer. I liked how we shared
the same traditional French spelling of our first name.
She consoled me with her message of hope and forgiveness. Somewhere along the line, I wrote a long wish list
on fine hotel stationary, including that I wanted to go on
cruise to Alaska and to attend one of Ms. Williamson's
conferences someday.

Within a week I received an email entitled: "Miracles
at Sea: A Cruise to Alaska with Marianne Williamson."

Listen, you *know* I went on *that* cruise.

In fact, just a few days before I received the providential email, at my hotel I met a friendly gentleman from far-off British Columbia (from where the cruise would depart). A few weeks later he hosted a special dinner party in Vancouver in my honor to introduce me to his many artist and foodie friends. It was all part of the positive turn: breaking out of the negative, dark box.

Marianne Williamson facilitated a class during the cruise through the spectacular glaciers and waterways of Alaska. It was not very Catholic, theologically, and I do not recommend her books now, but I believe God used the cruise to help me "where I was at" during this period. Marianne and I connected—I was able to spend quality time with her. She was flabbergasted by Luke's abrupt discarding of me.

And although I did not know there was still much suffering in store for me over the next twelve years, that carefree summer was a significant turn onto a new, long path to my return, finally, into the arms of Jesus.

I also met a woman named Martha on this cruise. She happened to live less than a mile from my brother, who resided in a city a few hours away. Martha and I became close friends, although she had a difficult personality. I visited her frequently, and naturally, spent time with my brother and his young family. My brother, who is only a year older than I am, was about to undergo his own personal trial: the tragic and sudden loss of his wife to a terminal illness.

Fewer than six months after the cruise, I was still lonely and dissatisfied with life; I felt I had little family support. When my brother invited me to move in with him temporarily, I accepted.

I began homeschooling his son and essentially tele-commuting for a start-up company supplemented with frequent long drives back and forth to their headquarters through a harrowing mountain pass.

For the first time in my life, I began listening to Christian music during these long drives; my brother's wife had given me a few CDs for Christmas the year before she passed away. I began to feel the love of Jesus. I felt his presence while listening and I felt at peace. The music was, in this sense, her sweet gift from heaven.

—◆◖◉

Other than my brother and Martha, I didn't know anyone in this new city (where I was not planning to live permanently). During a social event with Martha's adult daughter, however, I met my second husband.

I was not attracted to him at first, but we had an plethora of things in common. He had been married twice before. He was athletic, intelligent, and focused. He owned a growing business in a boomtown.

After a false start or two, we were seriously dating and considering marriage. When my contract job with the start-up ended, he invited me to move in with him and seek work in my brother's city—in effect, to settle there with him. I did.

Because of the nature of this book, it might seem to you as if I was constantly going from one bad relationship to another. In fact, it had been almost two decades since I entered my first civil marriage and there were long stretches over that period when I was not in a serious relationship. I was in my forties, not my twenties. Although still blinded by my unhealed codependency issues, I sincerely believed that I was being "cautious" entering into the second marriage. I was making sure he would be a good husband. I was not aware that my immoral behavior was clouding my judgement.

And because he also wanted to avoid his past marital

difficulties, I believed he was completely sincere when he claimed he would never get divorced and work through whatever challenges and difficulties faced us. He told me he wanted more children. "Divorce is not an option," was our own little mantra, and we repeated it often as we contemplated marriage.

Our relationship degenerated almost immediately after the wedding, despite stretches of good times. You nor I need endure the florid details. He left me, filed for divorce, and married another.

Not long afterwards, because he civilly married me without receiving an annulment to a previous Christian marriage, I received a Declaration of Invalidity due to a lack of canonical form.

In God's eyes I had never been married.

Emotionally, I was utterly devastated. The dashing of my hopes, the suppression of my true personality, and the years of mental anguish—even more than for any of the men before him—ruined me.

And, just before the divorce, I received discouraging news: I had breast cancer. Already slender, I lost thirty pounds, wasting away. My light was so dim that it almost flickered out. In this severely weakened physical state and vulnerable mental condition I still needed to find the reserves to recover from cancer surgery.

PART TWO

Alive Again

I am awake—I am alive again.
I can breath in the air with heart and soul:
Together they blend again.
*Living Waters, **Alive Again***

She gives me everything, and tenderly,
The kiss my lover brings, she brings to me.
*The Beatles, **And I Love Her***

The most faithful servants of the Blessed Virgin,
being her greatest favorites, receive from heaven
graces and favors, which are crosses.
Saint Louis de Montfort

I know a place where I can go, when I'm alone:
Into your arms, into your arms, I can go.
And if I should fall, I know I won't be alone anymore.
*The Lemonheads, **Into Your Arms***

Oh, Immaculate Mary, my life (every moment of it) and
my death (when, where, how) and my eternity belongs
totally to you. In all these things do whatever pleases you.
Saint Maximilian Kolbe, Martyr of Auschwitz

Come Holy Spirit

At first, a friend took me in for a few days during my recuperation—the breast cancer surgery was a success. I had adopted two male rescue cats during the second "marriage." Like me, they had been abused and had many health problems. I may not have survived without them during this difficult period. They provided acceptance, affection, and companionship. On most mornings, especially during the first few months, caring for the needs of my two "boys" was the only reason I got out of bed.

Then an acquaintance, Liz, who I had met through my volunteer work, saw me in a grocery store parking lot one day. I was emaciated and was not wearing any make up. She instantly deduced something was profoundly wrong and practically pounded down my door over the next few weeks to keep me involved with life outside my depressing apartment. She nicknamed me Gucci and we began texting and calling every night.

I had to sell my jewelry to pay bills, including small, seldom-worn pieces to have my hair done (I still had my priorities, Ladies). I gradually rebuilt my career after years out of the formal workplace. I was already very active in the Junior League in my new city, and I joined even more organizations.

My talents were well-suited to civic engagement. As a public relations professional, I collaborated with politicians, prominent business men and women—the movers and shakers. I was invited to take leadership roles for various charities. Within months of the divorce, and with little effort, I became well-connected to power brokers; I believe God was moving me quickly into a new "social sphere." Very quickly. I was certain the Holy Spirit was guiding me to be the woman He created me to be. I recall saying exactly this to myself at the time.

My brother had remarried so I was no longer a daily part of the lives of his children. My parents retired and lived hours away, as did my other siblings. The friends I made through community service became a *family of friends*, including some deeply committed non-denominational Christians. I began listening to their radio stations and learning about the Bible.

One television preacher who helped me climb out of the pit was Joel Osteen. I remember lying in bed, the covers over me, TV on, as he reassured me Jesus would bless me no matter how dark and difficult life was right now. God bless him. He helped me and numerous others during our darkest hours.

Although I was nearly two years away from a full reversion to the Catholic faith, something extraordinary happened. Through a series of connections from these new friendships, I found myself in a theater in Los Angeles praying with a group of serious Christians.

One of these new friends was a successful screenwriter and scientist, a devout Catholic named Glenda. She was close to members of this group of Christian Hollywood types—actors, producers, and writers—and had encouraged me to attend.

I remember feeling terrible that morning and not wanting to endure the five-hour trip alone to be part of this gathering. (I also had been suffering from heavy bleeding.) When I arrived I joined nearly a hundred people in a rented downtown theater. Before the prayer meeting began, I was introduced to a friend of Glenda's, an African American comedian named John. Around my age, he was full of life—the kind of person you just want to spend time with to soak up his goodness.

It was a well-kept, clean old place. The atmosphere felt cozy even though the dim yellow lights were on, as bygone theaters with burgundy-curtained walls often are. A prominent film producer walked up on stage and began to lead us in prayer. We all stood in front of our seats. John happened to be to my left and we all held hands. Music was playing. Things started to get *different* when John began shaking—jerking—and the vibrations traveled down his arm into my arm and shoulders. Eventually our prayer leader paused for a time of silence. John let go of my hand, turned to face me, then informed me that he had "a message" for me. I nodded, a tad confused by the sensory overload yet feeling his wonderful spirit.

Before I share what he told me that morning, please keep in mind that John and I had just met and that he knew nothing about me—not a single significant detail about my life. When he did begin to speak, his big brown eyes widened, his features became animated, and his voice rose and fell with prophetic timber and tremble, a message from God…

"You are a beautiful person with a kind heart and a gentle spirit. But people only see this," he gestured with a wave of one hand around my shoulders and head, indicating, in effect, my outward appearance, before continuing, emphasizing each word, *"You…are…not… alone.* People do not *understand the suffering* you have gone through. God sees your heart. God sees how your heart has been pulverized through psychological abuse by man after man in your life. I see your heart."

His words flowed out, over me, into me. It was overwhelming. I cannot remember everything he said. He spoke quickly, confidently. Having described my past, he pivoted to my future, continuing…

"With your voice and your story, you are going to help millions of women. You will be on a national stage and you will be an instrument of healing and hope. The first half of your life has been filled with abuse, agony, and suffering. Nobody truly gets it. Your latter years will be better than your former."

He went on for several minutes in this vein. He told me that I would write a book about my life. I did not understand how he could know details about the abuse in my past. Overall, his was an encouraging message. It was significant—it changed the trajectory of my thinking, which I did not know was possible. John's prophetic message from God was a palpable genesis of my eventual journey all the way home to Christ.

At the time I understood my Catholic faith poorly. Obviously, I had many spiritual and moral blind spots. I was certainly not familiar with the free-flowing ways of Evangelical prophecy. And although John's words and Spirit-led insight penetrated me, I was not able to fully receive it. I was not sure why he was predicting my future, what it meant, or what to do about it.

Remember how he used the word "pulverized" to describe what had been done to my heart by all those men over the decades? I was still in constant mental pain stemming from the most damaging relationship of my life, so my heart was not completely disposed to receive John's prophecy.

Still, I had a new friend, a profoundly dedicated Christian brother who wanted nothing from me except to help me live in God's will. We have kept in touch ever since that fateful prayer gathering. It is almost as if John was given a direct line to the vibrations of my heart. He continues to encourage me. "I see your heart," he repeats to me. "Your latter years will be better than your former."

I had a long way to go. If you are reading this book, and if you are relating to my story in any way, as the abuser, or the one abused, or perhaps as a younger soul who needs to turn away from or avoid a negative path, consider that you are now a part of John's prophecy that my life story would help others.

— ◀(◉

In the summer of that year I was heavily recruited to take a high level position in a large organization. Although by every measure I was a success compared to my predecessor, I was mistreated. The atmosphere was so bad that I dreaded going to work for the first time in my life. I eventually left in frustration.

During a career that spanned decades I had never experienced such an unprofessional culture. At least, by this point in my life, I was cognizant of what was occurring. I included this experience in this book because I know, for many readers, the abuse cycle is not restricted to family or romantic relationships. Many of you have suffered from employers, coworkers, and managers, often for years, under the horrible threat of losing your ability to support yourself or others financially.

I now consider that job another attempt by the evil one to crush my spirit.

— ◀(◉

If we backtrack just a little bit, several weeks after John's prophecy I also suffered one of the most emotionally painful traumas of my life. Earlier I mentioned having unusual bleeding before the encounter with John. In fact, I had been bleeding so severely that I had struggled for months. I was weak. I was out of commission for three weeks out of four. At social or work functions, the blood quickly seeped through and ruined many pieces of my wardrobe. Not long after John's prophecy I finally made an appointment with my OB-GYN.

My doctor, considered one of the best in the region, delivered her grim prognosis: she suspected that I had uterine cancer. She urged me to schedule a hysterectomy. I refused. Medical issues aside, I needed to preserve the ability to have a child. I did not want to imagine life without the potential for biological motherhood. Despite the crosses and Christian symbols tastefully placed about her office, my doctor was coldly impassive.

"You are past your child-bearing years. You don't have a husband. You don't need your uterus."

Her words struck me like a Mack truck. I was already condemning myself interiorly and now she was casually patronizing me. She did not care about me as a person or my psychological state. I felt lost, broken, and so alone. Alone beyond almost every reader's possible understanding of that word. No one had accompanied me to the office that day. The only other human being there, my doctor, was dismissing my motherhood with a shrug.

Discouraged, lonely, daily navigating difficult waters at work, physically exhausted after nine months due to the bleeding, and still unhealed and emotionally vulnerable from the divorce, I reluctantly consented to have surgery to remove my uterus.

A friend, a well-known politician, made sure I was treated in the finest hospital. My meals, including filet mignon, were prepared in similar fashion to a five-star restaurant. The room was rimmed with countless flower arrangements and cards. Nurses and attendants dressed in formal attire. There was a second bedroom next to my hospital room for potential overnight visitors. I enjoyed beautiful sunsets from my top floor window. I was in a drug-induced state; everyone and everything there was designed to further my physiological recovery. Yet darkness loomed beyond the high-end bubble.

After the surgery, the pathology lab confirmed that my womb had indeed been cancerous. Perhaps God had preserved me from an early grave or more physical suffering.

—◀⊙

Upon my release a dear friend took me into her home to take care of me for several days. I could barely move or climb out of bed. My relatives rarely visited. Time ticked by. Various forms of self-hatred set in. Over and over I mentally relived the years wasted on men who robbed me of having children. Robbed me of family itself—father with mother and child. I seethed with resentment. I was in physical and psychological pain, on the precipice of a mental breakdown.

Did God hate me?

Although the drugs dulled some of my physical pain, the emotional devastation had not been addressed. Because of my age, the permanent loss of my fertility did not strike any attendant or nurse as a meaningful mental health issue. During a follow-up appointment two weeks later, my doctor, finally recognizing that my physical recovery was being hampered by my psychological distress, frankly informed me, "I'm sorry, but we don't deal with that type of thing here."

Paradoxically, amidst this mental anguish, there was also a thread of release. It was as if the men with whom I had been intimate were somehow also removed along with my uterus. I felt almost virginal. It is difficult to put into words. I finally felt detachment from them—a psychological amputation. In one form or another, each had played upon my deep yearning to be a mother by promising to have children with me in a faithful marriage. Now, mysteriously, a significant part of their hold on me was gone.

It is a given that every reader has a different (hopefully perfectly chaste) sexual history. For those of you who have had one or more sexual partners, within or outside of marriage, you have experienced the invisible connection or bond created by sexual intercourse. A single experience can create the bond; this is part of God's design for human beings and it makes perfect sense within marriage. Outside of marriage, the connection can last for decades even if one does not have contact with the other person. Perhaps it is stronger in some women than in some men. It is invisible; it is real.

Somehow, my physical hysterectomy broke the psychological bonds with the men from my past. Now that I have returned to a full sacramental life of Catholic Christianity, I have been able to continue to heal the wounds with awareness and prayer. I have asked Jesus to bless the men I have been with and to release their connection to me in body, mind, and spirit. I invite you to do this too.

—❦

The morning after I was released from the hospital, something happened. I don't remember if I was dreaming or awake. I was gazing out the bedroom window to my left and through a few inches of open curtain felt the sun warming my face. I heard a heavenly, hopeful voice infuse me with this overwhelming goodness, a reality, and if it could be put into words, it would be, "Now you can adopt a child who you can love. There is a child out there who needs your love. This child wants to love you back."

There was a sweetness to the voice, to the sentiment itself, and it was consoling. I felt a tear roll down my cheek and I immediately was transported twelve years into my past, and remembered the other tear when I was on the surgical table.

Instantly my joy turned to anguish and self-hatred.

Dark thoughts pursued and harassed me.

God is punishing me. I took a life and now He is taking away my ability to create life.

In retrospect, I did not know about the Gospel story of the bleeding woman who had grasped Jesus' cloak and how He felt his "power go out" to heal her. I will always wonder: if I had known about this story, then perhaps I would have prayed before and after my devastating hysterectomy. Maybe things would have turned out differently. Maybe there was another doctor out there, someone who cared. A treatment that might have preserved my fertility. Maybe I could have prayed months earlier and received a miraculous healing before the cancer took hold?

I learned later that God was not punishing me, and I will share how this happened. But for the endless months that followed, I condemned myself. I could not go back in time to fix things, or redo or undo or avoid my tragedies, and going forward, without Jesus, there was little hope, only self-hatred and condemnation.

———◄(◉

In the time between the hysterectomy and my full return to the practice of my faith, I did not become romantically involved with anyone with one exception. By now most of the men interested in me were older, affluent, and prominent—and all of them were immature or sexually malformed (and often both). Users. They wanted, even lusted after me—my energy—I made them look good, but each was unwilling or incapable of fully committing to a relationship.

I dated a man I will call Richard for several months. He treated me with respect. Divorced, he promised me marriage and children while praising my Catholic faith although he was an Evangelical. It felt like I finally had a proper boyfriend for the first time since the divorce. On the morning of the Feast of the Assumption (I looked it up recently), I admitted to him over breakfast, "You've been doing all the right things. I know you love me."

After I said this, he muttered under his breath, just loud enough for me to hear, not realizing I *could* hear him, "It worked."

Huh? I was confused, although I did not show my inner reaction.

After that breakfast, I felt a strong intuition that I should not be with him, so I decided to stop seeing him. Simultaneously, he ghosted the relationship (ceased all texting and calls).

The following Sunday I experienced this very odd, strong pull to visit a particular bookstore although I did not plan to buy a book. Although many people were in the store, sitting directly in front of me at the cafe was a close friend of my now former boyfriend. I could not miss him. He was a Protestant minister, and a strong, kind-hearted man. He invited me to sit and I ordered an orange fizz.

He informed me bluntly, "Although Richard is my best friend, the problems you are experiencing have happened before. He is seriously messed up. Count it as a blessing that you are no longer with him."

The meeting was a divine appointment, and this man

of God spoke for God to keep another dangerous man out of my life.

Richard's utterance, "It worked," represented another charade, another long-term act by another phony Christian to drain my light and silence my voice.

The following week I went for a pedicure with a Christian friend: a tall, elegant woman named Margie. Although strongly anti-Catholic, she actually was employed by a Catholic foundation that supported a downtown woman's shelter. She was extremely faithful in her "Four Square" love of Jesus. As girls do, I shared with her what had happened with Richard while we were being pampered. Margie offered to pray over me; we had prayed together before. This time, standing next to our cars in the parking lot outside the salon, I felt something happen to me inside as she placed her hands on me. This was different. When we were done she gave me a big hug.

Shortly after I returned to my apartment that afternoon, I rushed into the bathroom and began vomiting violently. Strange thick black bile came out. It was like an erupting volcano, a kind of physical deliverance from evil. Ultimately, I felt "cleared" of something.

I am not a spiritual expert, so I cannot claim for certain that I was being delivered or released from harassment or oppression by evil spirits, but I did feel different—and better.

Angelica

Please recall how God gently led me (without my aware-ness of His unfathomable plans) to seek out and join civic organizations during this period after my second civil divorce. God moved many pieces on the chess board to nudge me to exactly the right place. By way of these civic connections, I was invited to be on the board of a local museum. At a museum event I met a woman who told me about a Catholic business group that met monthly to listen to faith-based speakers. I joined to connect with other Catholic professionals and to learn about my faith.

I was not cognizant or capable of discerning differ-ences between so-called liberal or orthodox Catholicism at the time (perhaps because I was a unique amalgam of both); it turned out this particular organization was quite faithful to authentic Catholic spirituality. I was soon invited to join their board of directors as well. Shock-ingly, it was the first fully Catholic organization I had been a part of since childhood—and Jesus was planning to use it to change my life rapidly and irreversibly.

And like a chess piece I was finally moved to the precisely correct square in September of 2015. I recall looking forward to hearing the featured speaker of our monthly breakfast meeting. His name was Bear Woznick and his experiences paralleled mine, although he was sixteen years older and a father of four. We shared many mutual interests, especially all things having to do with the ocean and its mysterious, dangerous, and sometimes comforting depths. As it happened, even though there were a hundred people gathered there, I sat directly in front of the podium at the restaurant where he gave his presentation. I was close enough to see the details of his hand-carved shark's tooth necklace and the hint of the Islander tribal tattoos peaking out from his open shirt.

Although born in the Midwest, he was a professional surfer who exuded an understated Hawaiian swagger. Sun-and-salt-kissed blond, neither tall nor short in stature, his stoutly muscular physique exuded strength. He spoke with authority, the voice of a calmly excited father. His love for theology, orthodoxy, and everything Catholic shines through and penetrates. I enjoyed his talk and I felt uplifted and energized.

I asked during the Q-and-A if he had ever gone free-diving. At my expense he rolled his eyes and groaned, "I don't like holding my breath…" to a burst of laughter from the audience, then smiled kindly.

Afterwards I purchased his book and approached him for an autograph. We began emailing and having spiritually-based phone conversations within days. This was another first—a faithful, fatherly, completely devout Catholic man concerned only for my best interests, and like John (the comedian who received a prophecy about me in the Los Angeles theater), Bear was the antithesis of the selfish men from my past.

Also like John, he strongly encouraged me to write my story. During one of our very first conversations, he shared that during his presentation he felt like I was the only person in the entire restaurant. He could feel the Holy Spirit vibrating within me and that my soul was bright shining as the sun. He sensed deeply that God had an extraordinary plan for my life going forward. He adamantly reinforced what John had prophesied: that the sufferings of my life had the potential to help many people, especially women.

Bear was a kind of "second" prophet through whom

God was impressing upon me to be a light to others.

—⟨◎

Do you remember how I sold my jewelry to pay my hairstylist in the wake of the divorce? And how God worked through my friend Margie to pray over me after a pedicure two weeks before I attended Bear's presentation? Gentlemen readers, please be patient with my girlie-girl-ness, but God continued to work through my, well, girlie-girl-ness.

God was now playing speed chess with my life like in those movies where you see players hitting clocks in Central Park. Exactly one week after hearing Bear, I met with a woman named Amy, a salon esthetician. A mutual acquaintance had recommended her, so we did not know each other well. I had spent six months trying to reach her. For some reason, I yearned to visit with her. I finally was able to confirm an appointment for a facial just after hearing Bear's talk.

I firmly believe, in retrospect, the evil one had been trying to keep us apart. Amy had been let go from one of the city's most notoriously catty and prestigious salons because, well, she was too kind and talented. She had started her own salon in the interim, which is one of the reasons why I had difficulty locating her.

You would love Amy. She is a petite woman with light cocoa-colored skin, a wonderful smile, and a sweet way about her. Imagine this beautiful lady standing next to me while I reclined on the table, peach-toned facial cream on my face, my neck muscles losing tension slowly. Relaxed, I told her about my ongoing nightmare at the college where I was still employed. We both found the parallels interesting when she then shared about the persecution she had suffered at the other salon—how gossipy, cold-hearted coworkers had singled her out and driven her away. I related. There were so many parallels in our experiences. Trusting her more, I began sharing details about what had just happened with Bear at the Catholic business association.

She gently evangelized me by talking comfortably about God as if it was completely normal. "We all have a divine purpose," she assured me. She considered her new salon an example of this principle. She told me her clients each walked away with a blessing. She had suffered negative experiences at the "prestigious" salon before starting her own establishment to help others. God had found a way to combine her talents with her calling to influence her clients' lives. In fact, without them realizing it, following the promptings of the Holy Spirit, she prayed over many of them.

Amy knew from experience God can use the suffering, difficulties, or challenges in our lives to bring about good—just as the crucifixion preceded the resurrection. She suggested that the next chapter in our lives would be a positive surprise from God even if it was scary.

At one point she asked me to say the holy name of Jesus.

"Jesus," I whispered. "Jesus."

I told her about John's prophecy in the theater "church" in Los Angeles a year and a half earlier and how Bear also had a premonition of my potential to help others.

Then…

Without realizing it, Amy brought me back to the Catholic Church forever. She did this by praying over me, lightly touching her hand on my forehead while praying in tongues very softly at the same time. I felt the Holy Spirit in my body and in my mind.

It felt so incredibly good. It felt right.

She was adamant. "Bear is a messenger from God in your life and the evil one has been using that manager at your job to make you miserable. I am here to tell you that I am the third messenger from God after John and Bear. You need to tell your story. I can feel it."

As the minutes ticked by and the Holy Spirit worked through both of us, it became clear to Amy that the challenges we overcame to meet after six months had definitely contained an element of spiritual warfare. This was September. Remember that August 15 (Feast of the Assumption) was the last day I saw Richard (which was providentially confirmed when I ran into his pastor at the bookstore). Then I had vomited black bile after Margie prayed over me in the parking lot while discerning a strong sense of release from demonic oppression. All of these events occurred in rapid succession in fewer than three weeks before hearing Bear and praying with Amy.

The Holy Spirit was stripping away the dark elements in my life.

Amy, which can be translated, "loving friend," and is an ancient title for Our Lady (Mother Most Amiable), was bringing the supernatural light back into my life.

You have to understand, because of *the way* Amy was praying over me (while in the process of giving me a facial!) and speaking so freely about God, spiritual warfare, prophecy, and the faith, I just assumed she was an evangelical Protestant. When I asked her where she attended services, I was surprised when she told me she and her husband were Catholic, and not merely Catholic, but *charismatic* Catholics.

It was no coincidence that I had first heard the term *charismatic* during a phone call with Bear just before meeting with Amy. He had been miraculously healed of a back ailment at a Catholic charismatic healing service during his own journey back to the full sacramental life.

Amy then shared information about a special Mass for charismatics at a nearby Catholic church and encouraged me to attend. It sounded like all the best parts of Protestant fervor combined with the best of the depths of Catholicism. I was thrilled!

"Is this for real?" I asked her, my eyes blinking from beneath the mask. She nodded and smiled sweetly.

It was as if the heavens were opening above me, calling me to be a part of this charismatic Mass.

When I attended this Mass the following weekend, I came back to the Catholic Church for good. On fire, fully, forever, and always, and I will never leave her again. Like the prodigal daughter, I had returned, and the Father ran out to embrace me. I was back in the full practice of my faith completely for the first time in three and a half decades, since I was a little girl clinging onto my mother's arm at Sunday Mass. Somehow I had survived a dysfunctional childhood, an endless succession of abusive relationships, civil divorces, constant emotional distress, suicidal desires, occult influences, the sins of others against me and my sins against others, cancers, and codependencies.

Checkmate.

—◀◉

Someone once told me that in our culture, every person older than twenty who is still practicing the faith is a convert in one way or another. I later discovered I am considered a "revert," a newly-coined Catholic term. A revert is someone who was raised in the Catholic faith during childhood and at some point stopped practicing the faith and stopped believing Catholicism is real or true to some degree before returning after years away to full participation in the sacraments and acceptance in heart and mind that Jesus really does act and speak the truth through His one holy Church.

I would not be surprised if most adults attending any given Catholic church are reverts to some degree, so if you decide to follow me back, you will not be alone.

And most of the wonderful Catholics who influenced me during my reversion were themselves reverts. (You still have a few more to meet!) I believe a significant portion of our generation of Catholics attending Sunday Mass have likely been away from the sacraments for various lengths of time.

It is also crucial for you to keep in mind what happened with Amy as well. I needed someone to guide me; allow me to be your Amy, your "loving friend." In the beginning, the important thing is to bring yourself back into the presence of Christ with an open heart—with an open mind. A deeper understanding of specific teachings—the beautiful thirst to learn about your savior, Jesus Christ—will be given to you. Your mind will be opened to the truths after you decide to change your orientation *with action.*

Actions can be simple. Talk to Jesus right now. Pray, "Jesus, help me." Drive to a nearby Catholic Church and spend time with Jesus in front of the tabernacle. He is there, waiting for you (and I don't mean just symbolically—He is *really* there). Just sit and let Him leave messages in your heart. Talk to your priest or minister, or to a believer you trust, about your need to have a close friendship with God.

If you were baptized into the Catholic faith as a baby (or anytime in the past), you can also begin by going to Confession at your local parish. The schedules are listed online nowadays. Then you can start receiving Holy Communion at Mass right away. If you want to become a Catholic, every parish has an RCIA program designed to bring non-Catholics into the fullness of the faith.

I invite you to listen, really listen, to this promise Jesus made:

Come to me all you who are weary and burdened and I will give you rest. Take up my yoke and learn from me because I am gentle and humble of heart. You will find rest for your souls because my yoke is easy and my burden is light. (Matthew 11:28-30)

And,

I tell you this so that you may have joy and that your joy may be complete. (Matthew 15: 9-11)

You have nothing to lose but your loneliness, toxic relationship patterns, unhappiness and internal conflicts. You will have complete joy. You have everything to gain: serenity in the midst of hardship, true happiness, friendship with God, Mary, and the saints, and the best human relationships you have ever known. As for me, I will forever speak the holy name of Jesus. Amen.

—❦—

Let me be clear. My reversion started two years before I began writing this book. Lingering issues in my life were real and did not suddenly disappear. I had suppressed very serious traumatic emotions and survived decades of codependent abuse and malformed decision-making, as you know from taking this journey with me. My reversion was *the beginning* of an internal battle because God wanted deeper healing for me. Opening my heart to Him during my reversion stirred the pot, and as you will see, led me to a place of sadness.

Next I will relate some of my experiences, good and not so good, with the charismatics, as well as more specifics about how I learned about my faith. After my encounter with the Holy Spirit through Amy, I had a long way to go, including a profoundly transforming sacramental experience in the spring of 2016.

———◄◖

The Charismatic Mass was actually two events consisting of a Sunday Mass attended primarily by members of the large parish charismatic group followed by a Praise and Worship hour. What distinguished the Mass itself was how every worshiper sang with enthusiasm. It was striking to hear and participate with men and women, children and teenagers, and seasoned citizens belting out full-throated hymns! Here I was, for the first time as a Catholic, among people who clearly made knowing and following Jesus Christ the highest priority of their lives.

The Praise and Worship hour featured, as you can guess, praise and worship, mostly through singing and brief preaching. It had been led for decades by an elderly couple who were now in their eighties. Some people raised their hands in the air and prayed in tongues—an ancient, mysterious practice described in the Acts of the Apostles whereby the Holy Spirit is thought to speak through a person in alternative, often unrecognizable, languages (this is what Amy had done at her salon).

A large amount of time was set aside for individual prayer and discernment. At every service people were invited to go to the front to be "prayed over." This consisted of leaders and a few others gently placing their hands on a particular person while praying out loud, speaking words of spiritual encouragement, asking for healing, and usually sharing what they felt God was saying to them regarding that person.

Often people would be "slain in the spirit" while

being prayed over. This is when a person would lose consciousness or fall asleep, actually falling back into a restful state. (Someone in the small group would be responsible to catch the person being "slain.") This happened to me several times. Overall, these individual prayer sessions placed an emphasis on asking the Holy Spirit for healing, guidance, and power (grace). The goal and "feel" of the hour was gentleness, helpfulness, and prayerfulness tailored to individual needs.

The church itself where we met was not in what would be considered a good neighborhood. There was gang activity in the area. I saw hardened gang members reduced to tears at our meetings. I witnessed the miraculous healing of physical ailments and emotional traumas. Through these humble believers, God was acting in powerful, sometimes dramatic, and often obvious ways.

I was so on fire for the Eucharist, which I now knew to be the real presence of Jesus, that for a time I attended evening Mass at another parish after going to the Charismatic Mass so I could receive my Lord twice on Sunday (receiving twice is allowed by the Catholic Church, by the way).

Once again, during the meetings, people I did not know well encouraged and even implored me to write my life story. For example, there was one leader, an ordained deacon who always addressed me, "Hello Woman of God!" I believe he saw my childlike trust in the Lord.

The Holy Spirit inspired him to tell me, "You have a message for others to help heal the brokenhearted."

Attending the Charismatic Mass and prayer hour coincided with a powerful internal thirst to learn everything about the faith. I began watching Catholic (and Protestant) television virtually all the time—especially

EWTN—and it seemed like every time I turned on a program there was a lesson personally designed for me. God spoke to me through my TV.

Catholic and Christian television personalities were my daily evangelists. With a friend I also watched Oprah Winfrey's Super Soul Sunday, which occasionally featured priests and nuns; this and other shows contributed to my development. I also listened to Christian music in my car, turning it into a kind of little church. I began reading the Bible and devoured Christian and Catholic books.

I especially found myself taking a crash course on the beauties and wonders of Catholicism. I am still learning; Catholics who have practiced for decades have since confirmed to me that the joy of learning about the faith never goes away. From other converts and reverts I have discovered that this thirst to learn is a gift and is commonplace; it will be given to you when you return as well.

And I have to admit that I became more than a little angry and confused about these treasures never being taught to me or virtually anyone else in the Catholic Church under the age of sixty. We've been duped! There is much needless heartache and suffering we could have been spared—and so much peace and joy we could have enjoyed!

One woman I met through the charismatic group was very clear with me. "Jesus is your spouse. Jesus is your lover. Right now you don't need to have a man or romance in your life. You've been baptized in the Holy Spirit. This is a period that Jesus wants to use to draw you closer to Him by reading his Word and spending time with Him in prayer. Elevate your spiritual experience with Jesus."

I took her advice. I created a comfortable consoling

spiritual cocoon. From the outside looking in, I must have appeared to be in isolation. For me, though, I was with Jesus. For these five months when I was in my Jesus cocoon He was preparing me for a powerful supernatural—and sacramental—experience.

I mentioned earlier that I began to feel a profound, gnawing sadness and also a sense of contradiction. I had been attending two Masses every Sunday. I was watching Mass on television on most weekdays. I was now forming friendships with on-fire Catholics. I was in my Jesus cocoon, gulping down spiritual truth directly from the spigot.

And all these things were stirring the pot. I could not avoid thinking about my past. Of course I realized God had not intended me to be with these harmful men and in context, the civil divorces had been good things—the spiritual equivalent, in God's eyes, of ending harmful relationships with long-term *boyfriends*. I am a child of God. I deserve to be cherished and loved and adored. These men and my past sins were a contradiction.

I use this word, *stuffed,* to describe what I had done with these issues. I had stuffed that pain and hurt deep inside. My propensity is to internalize traumatic events, to ignore them. As I shared earlier, I used perfectionism to mask my profound brokenness. These traumas had manifested in unhealthy decisions and relationships. I realized that I would also sabotage relationships, including friendships—it was easier to keep even good people at arm's length because it was so difficult to trust anyone.

These things, these dark realities, were still there, deep inside and my reversion to Catholicism and new-found closeness to Jesus were bringing them out.

I often imagined carrying these multiple crosses on my shoulders, so my joy attending the Masses and prayer meetings was tinged with a growing sense of dread. This began to manifest in an uneasiness and even negative emotions I felt while driving to the Charismatic Mass. I began to realize that for all the good that was going on during the prayer hour, there were also evil spirits at work, which I could sense. (I believe I have always been sensitive to spiritual realities, although I was ignorant of the details and theology.) In simple terms, something was making me feel bad.

It was weird. After several months of feeling so good about returning to my faith, things had changed. Abortion is a frequent topic in Catholic circles and on Catholic television and radio. The language used is not always sensitive to the damage abortion does to women. Even prayer intentions to end abortion at Mass seemed like little daggers in my heart. I felt judged. Maybe I was being judged. I knew I had been condemning myself since it happened. If you have had or participated in an abortion, perhaps you understand how I felt (and still sometimes feel). Of all the things I had stuffed down, this was the biggest. This was the one aspect of my past I did not think about and had avoided thinking about for many years. My lifelong habit and practice was to *not deal with issues*.

And my issues, because of my reversion and how negatively they were making me feel, were imposing themselves, forcing me to deal with them.

Now there was one priest in a nearby parish who God chose to help me deal with the darkness—to help me heal. Father Bert Mello was an older man who for decades had lived a life of sex, drugs and rock 'n roll so wild that it would have made Saint Augustine blush. Like me, he had been divorced and had experienced his own dramatic reversion. Not long after his return to the sacraments, he heard the call to the priesthood *in his early fifties*. Now in his sixties, he had been recently ordained and assigned to a nearby parish.

One of my best friends, Rita, herself a revert, told me about Father Bert and I was consoled by his hold-nothing-back life story and inspired preaching on You-Tube. I finally met him on December 8, 2015, the Feast of the Immaculate Conception. Rita made a point of introducing me to him after Mass. We both embarrassed her by going on and on about how wonderful she was!

Father Bert connected with me right away, perhaps because he is a little boy at heart and his faith reflects this. He was two weeks away from being reassigned to a church two hours from where I resided, so it was a small miracle I met him before he left. With the exception of another man God planned for me to meet months later, Father Bert was destined to become the most important man in my entire life.

───◀(◉

It should be no surprise to any reader that I had not been to Confession since early childhood. Even during the months after my reversion, I was not told that I needed to confess my sins and receive absolution before receiving Communion. The Church does a tragically neglectful job, even for Catholics who attend Mass regularly, "marketing" the amazing sacrament of healing and forgiveness called the Sacrament of Reconciliation (also known as Confession). Not one person in the Charismatic group had suggested I go to Confession. Perhaps I heard about Confession on EWTN or through my reading—I don't remember, but the deep sadness, dread, and spiritual discomfort I was experiencing, after spending many months in the "spiritual cocoon" with Jesus, was compelling me to go.

I wanted to go face-to-face, as an adult woman. In the deepest part of myself, I knew it had to be with Father Bert. I hoped, because of his own past, that he would not judge me. Like most who have been away from Confession for years or decades, I was afraid of his reaction.

I later discovered these baseless fears were caused in part by my being such a newbie and are typical of the evil one's attempt to deter people from receiving God's mercy. I should add that the campfire stories of ornery priests yelling at people in confessionals in the olden days either were never true or were gross exaggerations; nowadays it is impossible to find a priest who is not kind, welcoming, and specially trained for the kinds of issues modern Catholics bring to them.

Now that Father Bert and I knew each other, it was relatively easy to schedule an appointment for a Wednesday afternoon at his new parish.

━━◀◉

You are not going to believe this, but before I tell you about what happened when I went to meet with Father Bert, you should know that I am dictating this chapter from a hospital bed. They found a cancerous tumor the size of a softball in my abdomen and last night into the wee hours of the morning I received my first course of chemotherapy.

It is surreal to write such a thing, I know. Hopefully the chemo will work and I will have a long life ahead of me. Because the tumor is compromising my digestive system and pushing against lower back muscles, I can barely walk or sleep, even while under heavy pain medication. I have been in excruciating physical pain for over fourteen days—all this before the legendarily nasty side effects of the chemo begin in about a week.

Just so you know.

—◀◖

Where were we? Before meeting with Father Bert I prepared thoroughly for what is called a "lifetime Confession" by taking comprehensive notes in the days beforehand; he did not tell me to do this, but I sensed that it was needed.

Father Bert's parish has a large grounds consisting of several acres, including a grammar school, athletic fields, and the church itself all nestled in a relatively nice mixed-ethnicity neighborhood in a big city known nationally for its advanced state of decay. He is the pastor and the lone priest. He had been there for only a few weeks when I drove down to meet him, so the fairly comprehensive rejuvenation of the campus he has spearheaded had not begun.

He is a stout, bald man with the face of a boxer; he loves to snack on sweets. He shuffles along, clearly in some kind of pain he never brings up—a remnant from his party days. Every guest and visitor is offered candy and drinks. Everyone gets an affectionate bear hug from Father! If he were not so obviously friendly and lovable, his manner would be considered gruff. Even before his conversion he was the guy everybody wanted to be around, the life of the party, and known for his big heart.

He has two offices: a large one with a desk and the usual appointments (supplemented with ample pictures and statues of Jesus, Mary, angels, and saints) and another, cozier room where he spends time meeting with people. This meeting room has two plush leather love seats and an easy chair which circle a small coffee table (for the snacks!). There are shelves and cases filled with books; beautiful Catholic art is everywhere in hodgepodge fashion.

After the greeting, hug, and a bit of ambling small talk, he led me to this peaceful, comfortable room. Instead of sitting across from each other, we both sat on the nearest corners of the love seats, turning slightly to face one another.

I didn't know how to begin. I fumbled with my notes. He carefully placed his stole (a band of thin material priests may don while hearing Confessions) around his compact neck, took my little girl hands into his warm, thick-fingers, looked me in the eye and said, matter-of-factly, "Just start."

And so that is how I began to confess my sins, sorting them by the decade, beginning with my teenage years. It poured out of me for hours. Father spoke rarely, except to gently encourage me to keep going, all the while holding my gaze and my hand. As a perfect *alter christus*, another Christ, he looked upon me with mercy and empathy. I felt loved. I felt safe. He listened.

You know what I told Father Bert because you just read it yourself.

I was not planning to tell him about my child and what I had done. I had not had the courage or honesty or whatever was needed to write it in my notes. I had not told a living human being what I had done. I had not told God. But the minutes turned into hours in that comfortable room in Father Bert's rectory as I gradually worked my way toward that time of my life.

When I reached that point, I felt ambivalently compelled to tell him, but I could only manage to say so indirectly by describing the circumstances. He understood. He broke his silence. "Oh, Marianne, you have been beating yourself up about this for years, haven't you?" His tone was filled with concern.

I nodded through my tears. He waited patiently for me to gather myself.

"You have to confess it. You have to say the words," he advised, always gentle in his firmness, his gravelly voice just above a whisper.

A long, long silence ensued. He held my hands. I looked up and saw Mercy.

I spoke the words.

And then we went to my next sin, to the next decade of my life, until the sun began to gently embrace the horizon, until there were no more sins to tell. I did not know the Act of Contrition; Father Bert, anticipating this, gave me a booklet which contained the traditional prayer.

"Oh my God, I am heartfully sorry for having offended thee," I began, "and I detest all my sins because of thy just punishment, but most of all because they have offended thee my God, Who art all good and deserving of all my love. I firmly resolve, with the help of thy grace, to sin no more and to avoid the near occasion of sin. Amen."

Father gave me absolution by making the Sign of the Cross over me and placing his warm hands on my head as he spoke, "God the Father of Mercies, through the death and resurrection of his Son has reconciled the world to himself and sent the Holy Spirit among us for the forgiveness of sins. Through the ministry of the Church may God give you pardon and peace, *and I absolve you from your sins* in the name of the Father, and of the Son, and of the Holy Spirit."

"Amen," I mumbled, my body filling with warmth.

My penance was to pray a single Our Father.

Here is what I prayed, interiorly, like a little child:

Our Father, who art in heaven, hallowed by thy name. Thy kingdom come, thy will be done, on earth as it is in heaven. Give us this day our daily bread and forgive us our trespasses as we forgive those who trespass against us. Lead us not into temptation and deliver us from evil, Amen.

My lifetime Confession was finished! I felt as light as a feather and happy and wrung out like a damp cloth all at the same time. And at peace. I am not sure if there were any more tears left in my whole body.

But Father Bert was not finished! With the verve of a little kid opening gifts on Christmas morning, he produced his bronze chrism oil container and proceeded to give me the Sacrament of the Sick, which heals body and soul.

Fragrant holy oil still reflecting a pleasant sheen upon my hands from this beautiful sacrament, he took out his pix, carefully opened it, and offered me Holy Communion. After a few required preparatory prayers...

"Lord I am not worthy that you should enter under my roof," I was finally able to speak, humbly and truthfully, "but only say the word and my soul shall be healed."

"The Body of Christ," Father Bert said, holding up the Host before my gaze, looking through it to me.

"Amen."

He placed the Eucharist on my tongue.

After several minutes of talking directly to Jesus inside me, I opened my eyes. Father explained that the absolution I had just received in Confession was not mere forgiveness of sins (after all, Jesus atoned for all sins for all time on the Cross), but that it was an actual transformation or restoration of my soul to a sinless state—the same state that I was in on the day of my baptism as a baby. Catholics call this the "state of grace."

This was true. I felt it. I was not the same person as I was before I received absolution. It is difficult for people to accept, but as Father Bert explained, God had *forgotten* my sins and *cleansed* my soul (me!) completely.

My sins were *no more*.

The Holy Communion—the body, blood, soul and divinity of Jesus I consumed into my body while in my state of grace—it was, well, more *more*.

Everyone—you, the people you love, your enemies, everyone you know—should experience the triple miracle of grace that Father Bert gave me: the Sacrament of Reconciliation, the Sacrament of the Sick, and the Sacrament of Holy Communion.

—◄(◎

Not long after that, a few months later, I was standing in my bedroom next to my bed, feeling tearful and morose because my parents, now in their eighties, were both ill—my father with Alzheimers and my mother with various ailments. They lived nearby and she was beginning to struggle with communicating to me during many of my daily visits. I had a strong premonition that my mother's earthly time was growing short. I needed her, but she was going to leave me. This realization was devastating.

Now back in my own apartment, in my bedroom, I was distraught. "I really need a mom. I really need my Mommy," I kept whispering to myself through the anguish. My face was puffy from the hours of weeping. Across the bed, I saw the three wooden crosses I keep on my wall. Tears streamed down my cheeks onto my nightgown.

Then the presence of a person was in my room. It

was exactly as if you, a real person, were standing right next to me, only invisible. This person next to me was a woman. She was Mary, the mother of God.

"You are my daughter," she told me.

Then I felt her warm embrace. I was enveloped—hugged—with spiritual warmth.

When you need your mother, you want to feel nurtured, and Mary nurtured me that evening.

—❧

God is about multiplication. Instead of limiting Jesus, the Father expanded Him by giving Other Christs—his priests, Father Berts—with the power to convert, heal, absolve, and restore his children (us) by the hundreds of millions. Real healing is available for the abused, codependency, and mistakes. The Gospels show Jesus spending the greatest portion of his time loving his friends, praying, fasting, healing, and forgiving sins. Instead of limiting Himself to heaven, He is truly with us, as True God and True man, in the Eucharist, in the little House of Gold (the tabernacle where Holy Communion is stored between Masses) in every Catholic Church to the ends of the earth, so we can enjoy a one-flesh union with Him more intimate than sexual intercourse.

If you do this, if you follow me home or into the Catholic Church, the emotional suffering I have endured for decades and the physical agony coursing throughout my body over the past few weeks will have been worth it. Because I can be like Jesus. I have experienced the cross and the resurrection. When you see me, I want you to see His light because my light was His light all along. I am his little girl now. He loves his little girl. And she loves him.

My daughter also came to visit me. She was a child no older than seven. I do not remember when she came to me because it feels both recent and a long time ago and it might have been in a dream or it might have been a vision. None of that really matters to me.

I know she was real.

My daughter has dark hair like mine and was wearing a white dress with lace sleeves. She came up to me, stood in front of me, then reached both arms out to me.

"I forgive you and I understand, Mommy," she told me. "I'm okay."

I named her Angelica.

William

After my cleansing Confession with Father Bert, my internal orientation toward men was transformed. In addition to the graces from the sacrament, this was due in part to Father Bert's loving acceptance of me. I experienced a man's selfless, genuine kindness—truly, the love of Christ. As a priest he had sacrificed everything to serve the Kingdom of God—and to serve me in particular—he had made a total gift of himself as Jesus had done. That is the real meaning of celibacy that our culture has so much trouble understanding. Some people implicitly feel this about Catholic priests. Others, out of ignorance, pity or mock their total Christlike gift of self.

As for romantic relationships, I could see my situation clearly for the first time in, well, for the first time ever—so it became difficult to accept invitations from the superficial men who were still pursuing me. I was also quite aware that God had intervened earlier to end my relationship with Richard—and that the evil one had been sending men like him into my life to hurt me for decades.

I became deeply discouraged about my prospects for finding a truly Catholic man—at least one who would accept me as I really was, including my brokenness. Both of my "civil marriages" were invalid—annulled. I had never been married in God's eyes or my own. I was alone and still longed for true love. And I still held out hope against hope for motherhood through adoption—women my age all around me were having children, after all.

How does the saying go?

Let go and let God.

One evening, discouraged yet hopeful, I prayed, "Dear Lord, Please allow me to be with a man who will meet me where I'm at and love me as I am." I even wrote it down.

Then, around two weeks later, I found the courage to pray, "God, I give up. I'm not picking men anymore. I'm giving this to you. You find him for me."

I should have asked a long time ago.

Motivated by John's prophecy and my new charismatic friends' urgings that my life story could help many people, I began preliminary work on this autobiography, hoping it would help women and men, young and not so young. Remember Bear, the writer I met at the Catholic Professionals breakfast? We were still in touch. He encouraged me to attend a Catholic conference to meet with potential publishers. He was attending as well and promised to make introductions.

A few weeks beforehand, while making travel preparations, I heard these words very clearly, interiorly:

You are going to meet your husband there.

My response was not very holy.

"Yeah, right," I joked out loud. I even laughed. Fat chance.

Time passed by. For some reason I felt soul-sick while getting on the plane for the conference. I arrived a day early and along with some of the other attendees, toured a beautiful shrine dedicated to Saint Maximilian Kolbe, the priest-martyr of Auschwitz who gave up his life for a man with a family. I learned that he had dedicated his life to promoting Total Consecration to the Immaculate Heart of Mary. With great intimacy he addressed Our Lady as "the Immaculata," a reference to her Immaculate Conception. That is, if you are not Catholic or are like me before my reversion: Mary was conceived without Original Sin in her mother's womb in fitting preparation for her role as the mother of Jesus.

And the name of Mary's mother? Anne. My name, Marianne, is a combination of both. Knowing this consoles me.

As I would later learn, Saint Maximilian focused much of his teachings on Our Lady's unique relationship with the Holy Trinity: she is the daughter of the Father, the mother of the Son, and spouse of the Holy Spirit. From that perspective it is no wonder she can have such a powerful impact on our lives! I also learned that Saint Maximilian founded a spiritual association, the Militia Immaculata, which has millions of members worldwide. This visit was encouraging—and turned out to be a foreshadowing, as we shall see.

On the following day, the good spiritual vibes from the shrine wore off quickly. My uncharacteristically negative mood was not helped by interacting with a publisher who recommended I downplay the darker details of my life story (multiple civil divorces, the R-rated sexuality, the codependency and abuse) and instead focus on the "happy" parts of my conversion.

I simply could not shake a powerful compulsion to leave the conference early. Maybe it had something to do with the day of the year being the anniversary *of that day.* It was July 26th. Maybe it had *everything to do* with it being *that day.*

I now know there was intense spiritual warfare going on. I even called the airline to reschedule my flight home.

The evil one wanted me to leave.

God wanted me to stay.

Then the Holy Spirit gently maneuvered me into meeting a handful of wonderful Catholic women representing a group called WINE—Women in the New

Evangelization. Because of their warmth and enthusiasm I decided to stay. Their founder, Kelli Wahlquist, kept texting me as well, urging me spend time with them that evening. As a result I found myself with a dozen-plus attendees at an after party in the lobby outside the hotel bar.

And it was here that I met William, my first and only true love.

During our first conversation, we both felt as if there was an invisible wall between us. Even so, he was a good listener. My heart opened a little when he offered to drive me and some of the WINE gals back to our hotel. Someone snapped a photo, then he drove off.

All the ladies, who had seen me conversing with him at the party, immediately began asking me what I thought about him and if I liked him. They told me he was a good man.

Did they see something I don't?

The next morning, at a breakfast reception, I was moved when he asked me about my parents and wanted to know if they were okay. Both had been struggling with illness. He made a point of memorizing their names and promised to pray for them, especially to Saint Anthony. He was so genuine. A man asking about my parents was a first for me.

When the conference concluded he drove me to the airport. With traffic it was a long drive and I felt naturally comfortable opening up to him about my past, which is not like me.

After parking ("There's no way I'm dropped you off at the curb.") he offered me his free arm as we walked through the parking lot. He was courtly and protective. When we were required to cross several busy automobile and shuttle lanes to enter the terminal, he boldly took my hand, and in a way, I never let go.

Once inside the terminal, when a few service people treated and spoke to us as if we were married, it was more than a little jolting. *"Is your husband also checking a bag today?"*

We started texting and talking as soon as my plane landed. He began our first date by praying with me at Perpetual Adoration. Then we went to one of my favorite charity events, but not before he treated me to the best dirty martini I've ever had!

———❦———

William is a Catholic man so wonderful, kind, fun, faithful, passionate, prayerful, manly, and loving that I can still hardly believe he exists. He had always been a deeply faithful Catholic with a simple, very childlike faith. His excitement for life matches mine perfectly.

It was like we were two "halves" wandering the world not knowing we needed the other to be a "whole." According to him "we are tuning forks on one spiritual frequency." He pursued me brilliantly and I have told him many times, "You made me love you."

"Yup," he replies, making me laugh. My William is good at that.

Our hands fit perfectly together. Chaste his whole life, he is at once extremely affectionate and respectful, which really can happen, Ladies. Things occur—like supernatural lightning—when we go to Confession, pray the Rosary, and receive the Eucharist together (at least most of the time). When he looks into my eyes, we connect. He says I calm him in a way that only the Eucharist had done before meeting me; I marvel as his face relaxes and he becomes completely serene while he looks into my soul. I feel safe and loved in his arms.

William is all those things in the famous Bible verses

by Saint Paul when he describes what love really is. You know the one:

Love is patient, love is kind. It does not envy, it does not boast, it is not proud. It does not dishonor others, it is not self-seeking, it is not easily angered, it keeps no record of wrongs. Love does not delight in evil but rejoices in truth. It always protects, always trusts, always hopes, always perseveres. (Corinthians 13: 4-7)

I tell him so. He shakes his head but does not deny it. Okay, maybe he is a little bit proud.

He "leads with the Lord," which I now know is what I have always wanted. He has been deeply hurt in previous relationships as well, and tells me that he knew his whole life that I was coming. He says, "I knew my wife would have a sweet heart. That she would not have mean bone in her body."

On December 8th, the day I met Father Bert last year, William was on his knees before the Blessed Sacrament, praying for his future wife. He prayed for me every day when he received Holy Communion before he ever met me.

He calls me his angel.

—◀◉

And he does lead me. Do you recall how I visited the Saint Maximilian Kolbe Shrine the day before I met him? It turns out William had consecrated his heart to Immaculate Mary as a young man and was already a member of Kolbe's Militia Immaculata.

Being a member, he explained, was not about doing things and more about taking on a new state of being. This intrigued me, and a few months later, after a little bit of preparation, we went to an oceanfront beach as the sun rose to make my consecration.

It was on my fiftieth birthday.

What is the consecration? To consecrate is to "set aside for a holy purpose." Consecration to Immaculate Mary is giving yourself to Jesus through Mary as a way of setting yourself aside for their holy purpose. Everything in your life after your consecration—even sleeping—will be used by Our Lady to help you know and do the will of her son.

You can find out more on the Militia Immaculata website. I also recommend Father Michael Gaitley's wonderful book designed to help anyone prepare for the consecration, *33 Days to Morning Glory,* which is spreading like wildfire all over the world.

On the morning of my consecration, there was a whale frolicking in the water far off to the south, well beyond the breakers, her giant tail fin rising and falling, creating enormous splashes. Some inner knowing assured me it was female and that she was expecting.

"I just know she's pregnant," I assured my darling man.

To reach the water's edge we had to make our way down a steep cliff using a series of crisscrossing wooden steps. He set up a blanket and I sat upon a large driftwood log. I took off my sandals and scrunched my toes into the sand. We composed ourselves to pray. We held each other with our eyes before I looked out to the ocean and saw my whale. *Is she coming closer?*

Then chills ran through my entire body as I prayed the old-fashioned words of the formal consecration—the same words William had prayed years ago—giving myself entirely to Jesus through Mary. Here I was, exactly fifty years since the day I was born and I was taking a radical new spiritual path. I will never be the same.

You will never be the same, either, if you join us.

After a time, holding hands, we climbed back up the

stairs and then sat on a bench facing the surf to pray our first Rosary together as consecrated souls. Before we started, William agreed that the whale was indeed heading closer to shoreline and that she seemed to be heading north in our direction as well.

As we prayed a mother and daughter came up along the beachfront. The mother, neither young nor old, was wearing a white sun dress and the little girl was in a pink, flowery jumper. They were so beautiful, stepping along lightly, barely touching the sand, like butterflies. Picking up stones and shells. I could hear their laughter wafting up from below.

"Hail Mary, full of grace…" William prayed, and the little girl darted toward the water, laughing, happy. "Holy Mary, Mother of God…" I prayed, peace in my heart, happy.

Before we began our last decade, they came up the same steps we had climbed and strolled right by us. The four of us nodded and exchanged smiles.

The symbolism was undeniable. I turned to my best friend and thanked him.

"I am that little girl."

We then had breakfast in a modest little place facing the water, followed by a long stroll, arm-in-arm, along the boardwalk. We discussed our future life together—where to live, adopting children, possible career changes—all peppered with his nonstop wit and my laughter. I was so happy!

As we drove out of the parking lot across the road from the beach where I consecrated my heart to Mary, we were amazed to see that "our" whale had now come extremely close to the shore and was now aligned directly in front of the bench where we had prayed our first "consecrated" Rosary.

"Bye bye, Momma," I whispered.

Weeks later, on the Feast of the Immaculate Conception, with William's help, my mother and father consecrated their hearts to Mary as Militia Immaculata. If this cancer ever takes me—hopefully many years from now—we will all share this beautiful state of being in eternity.

———◀(◉

Other than Father Bert during my Confession, William became the only person I trusted enough to tell about Angelica. For weeks I dreaded sharing this part of my past with him.

One evening, very late at night, I told him I had done something very bad and asked him to guess. He could not. He just doesn't "see" me that way even though he knew everything else about my past.

I finally forced myself to tell him everything about what had happened and what I had done. He listened in complete silence, looking into me in that way of his.

"Do you still love me?" I asked like a little girl, never more vulnerable. "Will you kick me to the curb?"

He'll leave me—he will be gentle and kind about it but he will leave me and I will be by myself for the rest of my life.

The old Marianne was sure I had just lost him. I braced myself to wait for his rejection.

Yet he did not let me wait and he took my hands—just like Father Bert, he took my hands. Tears welled up in his eyes. He pulled me closer and touched his forehead to mine.

"I love you, I love you, I love you, I love you…" he repeated over and again. "I will always love you."

We held each other for a long time and mourned together.

Then I told him about how she came to visit me.

I told him her name.

Not long after, he encouraged me to write about it. What I could not admit to myself for many years I told Jesus through Father Bert. Then Jesus sent me William, as He promised He would. Now I am telling you.

———◀◖◎

Much time has passed. Now that William knows about Angelica, I trust him even more. After all, I asked God to send me someone who would accept me as I really am, and now I know for sure, beyond doubt, that he does.

Of course, before the cancer struck so suddenly we were planning to become engaged. I spent time and fell in love with his devoted father and holy mother, along with his closest friends; he has met mine and so our love has expanded into our extended families. Since my diagnosis he has been at my side completely, praying with me for a miraculous cure, coordinating my medical care, sleeping in the chair in my hospital room until the next morning—charming all the nurses, establishing a frank rapport with the doctors, and making sure I have every littlest tiny thing I need.

He was not the best caregiver at first—in part because he had to transition into that role overnight, but also because he was trying too hard. My friend Liz was able to give him a short course because her husband is recovering from eye cancer and she knows the ropes.

William is my rock. Sometimes my rock weeps with me, expressing our mutual sorrow beyond words.

Why now? Why did I get sick now, when I am finally happy, in love with Jesus, his Church and have this wonderful man in my life—the first truly good man who has ever loved me?

While most of what the world considers "romantic" is no longer possible for us, we are marveling, despite the pain and sorrow, at the deeper experience of love we are enjoying—true devotion. Because my immune system is compromised by the chemotherapy, it is even dangerous for us to kiss. We pray, always. We can still hold (sanitized) hands.

We talk when my mind is clear (and lately I have been able to cut back on the painkillers as the latest chemo round wears off). We receive Holy Communion together when the chaplain comes to my hospital room. When I have been at my apartment, William goes to daily Mass and brings the Body of Christ to me. The supernatural electricity remains.

"I don't care about what we don't have, Baby. I love just being with you," he assures me, matter-of-fact man.

I cherish my darling sweet William. I am so grateful for him. Through the fog of the medications and the chemo and the pain I can truly witness to you with all my being that holy Catholic men such as William really do exist.

The Ocean

Now you know how my journey took a beautiful and decisive turn for the better after my "life-time" Confession. William.

Even so, because of my current predicament, I feel obliged to share with you about the contraceptive pill, which is an artificially-manufactured ("man made" according the National Cancer Institute) hormone which suppresses ovulation as its primary action or effect. As you know, I began using the pill as a sixteen-year-old when my "friend" took me to Planned Parenthood after I started sleeping with Billy.

I have done my research; you can look up the medical facts yourself using the references supplied at the end. In addition to the disastrous moral and psychological contributions the pill made to the darker developments that my story tragically illuminates, the pill is a Class 1 carcinogen. That is the worst possible classification. You can Google it. Among other risks, women who use the pill are significantly more likely to contract (and die) from breast cancer, uterine cancer, and ovarian cancer.

Hello, my name is Marianne Collins, I was on the pill for years, and I have had all three of those cancers! I did not know about the astounding medical risks when I was on the pill. No doctor informed me. Planned Parenthood certainly did not tell me. I heard about these risks for the first time less than two years ago on EWTN, the Catholic television channel, during a show featuring a panel of doctors. If this is your first time finding out, too, no matter how old you are, I can fully empathize.

And make sure your doctor scans you for all three of those cancers!

If you take the pill, you are harming yourself. I was. If you are a man, now that you know the truth, if you allow or participate with the decision for your wife, daughter, or your girlfriend to take the pill, you are harming a woman for your own pleasure, selfishness, or mistaken sense of responsibility. Using the pill is the opposite of being "responsible."

After reading this passage, William asked me if I would have taken the pill had I known about these risks to my health. I admitted the truth. Given who I was at the time and how misguided I was (by my own decisions, by mistreatment or neglect by others, and by the general culture—I will let God figure that out) I believe I would have used the pill even if I had known the risks. It gave me what I wanted—it allowed me to sleep with men without being concerned about pregnancy. It facilitated immoral, non-marital relationships in the name of "love." Like so many women, I believed I had to sleep with a man to keep a man. All the men I was with had the same attitude—they expected it.

And, for me at least, on very rare instances, it allowed me to have sex for pleasure with men to whom I was not committed. I also mistakenly believed that my two "husbands" would eventually make good on their (false) promises to have children with me, and the pill was a means of giving them time to come around, or at least so I believed in my convoluted mindset.

Now for the really difficult part. It was not until after I shared my past with William (I hid nothing from him) that I discovered that a secondary medical effect of the contraceptive pill is to prevent a fertilized egg from attaching to the uterine wall. The pill suppresses ovulation but does not always prevent it. (This is intended to decrease the incidence of blood clots and aneurysms that killed many women before the dosage was reduced in the 1970s.)

Typically, a woman on the pill or a hormonal implant will still ovulate and possibly conceive a child one or more times per year, yet be unaware of a spontaneous miscarriage caused by this secondary effect of making the uterus a hostile environment for a recently conceived human being.

What all this means is that the pill is an abortifacient. A fertilized human egg is a complete, genetically unique human being, no matter how tiny. There is no sober medical or scientific debate about these facts—the pharmaceutical companies *have openly designed* the pill to have this abortifacient effect to make it *more effective in preventing births*. Thus these effects are clearly spelled out in their own medical literature. The pill is a form of chemical abortion; the science indicates it is likely responsible for an estimated four or five times more deaths than surgical abortion.

My friends, I was horrified and depressed when William gently informed me about these medical and scientific realities. It hit me hard, and despite his tenderness, I resented him, but only for a little while. As you probably have figured out, in addition to our amazing compatibility and our deeply mystical prayer connection, we hide nothing from each other, even when it hurts. We want to work through our issues, not ignore them. I did not want to go into denial now that I have been freed by the light and love of Jesus. On this earth I will never know for certain if I unknowingly conceived and lost children while I was on the pill. In the next life, however...

I have asked myself, *Is this latest cancer a punishment for my sins?*

William disagrees vehemently. Although my own cancers were and are almost certainly the result of taking the pill, he quickly points out that little children and all kinds of innocent people get cancer. It is a tragedy for every victim and their loved ones.

Theologically, he and Father Bert and all my learning about the Catholic faith (including my prayer with Jesus) assure me that God has absolved me completely. He cannot *remember* my sins. "I will forgive their evildoing and remember their sins no more." (Hebrews 8:13) As Father Bert tells me, after I am absolved in Confession, my soul is as pure, in terms of sin, as a little baptized baby's.

God does not remember. Yet, in my darker hours, *I remember.*

Dear Jesus, I did not know. I am so sorry!

I would not have used the pill if I had known it was also an abortifacient.

I am forcing myself to write this because I do not want to think about it. When I was in committed relationships and "married" those two men, I wanted to be a mom so much. I thought I was doing the right things with these men to become a mother. It is all so tragic.

William has prayed with me for God's ultimate mercy for all the children I may have conceived; that is why he told me the truth about the pill in the first place. This has given me consolation, as does my true love's clear-eyed yet understanding perspective. He does not judge me—he believes, as I do, that our generation and those who follow us today have been unknowingly abused and malformed by the sexual revolution. We act mostly out of ignorance. Consider how our government on virtually all levels, our educational institutions, Planned Parenthood, our female friends and our boyfriends, the drug companies, and (in many cases) even our parents all conspire to make certain our young ladies use the pill, contraceptive implants, and IUDs (all abortifacients). We really are immersed in what Pope Saint John Paul II called "the Culture of Death."

We need compassion, not judgement, and authentic, loving compassion includes being told the truth about what can harm us and others.

—❧∅

I am started to wonder if the chemo is working. My pain is getting worse, which I did not think was possible.

"I'm sorry," I tell William sometimes when no one else is around. This must be so difficult, taking care of me. I can't give him what he wants.

"Sorry for what, Baby Girl? You have nothing to be sorry for," he replies sweetly, knowing exactly for what. *For what we will never have.* Melting my heart.

This is the man Jesus chose for me.

The truth is I do not know how much time we have left together. Years? Months?

Yet Christ prepared me for this last year, although I did not fully realize it at the time. Late last summer, feeling fit, happy, and newly in love, already looking forward to decades together, William and I took a day trip to Carmel, California. We love visiting the Mission churches built by Spanish Franciscans beginning in the 1700s to serve the Native Americans.

Inside the Mission in Carmel we knelt together at the railing of the sanctuary with the sarcophagus of Saint Junípero Serra actually located in the floor just a yard in front of us. There are very old statues of the crucifixion scene behind the altar, portraying Our Lady and Saint John keeping vigil at the passion of Jesus.

While holding William's hand, I fell into a trance as

the scene before me opened up into three dimensions. I was not in the Mission church anymore, but right there "inside" the crucifixion, reliving the scene with Mary and John and Jesus. It was intensely sad.

Then I heard my Lord tell me, "This is your life now."

Afterwards, in the courtyard, when I shared what happened, William's eyes widened. Although he did not enter into the crucifixion scene like I had, he had an interior thought of his own: "This is your home now."

At the time, the interpretation of the messages seemed obvious. His "home" was with me. My "life" with him. Right? Isn't that what you would have thought? We were looking forward to decades of happiness together.

We were correct and mistaken at the same time. Any place I am now is William's home and he really is my life—so much my life that I cannot imagine life before him or without him. Yet not too long after that Mission revelation, my mother, who was already ailing and bedridden, took a turn for the worse. I had already been visiting her nearly every day after work. It was hurting my heart to watch her degenerate so quickly.

She lived in a large sunroom with my father at my brother's house. Dad is in his late eighties and suffers from Alzheimers, so his memory resets every thirty minutes or so. He is like a little boy (and sometimes he is a brat). Mostly, my parents still love each other very much. Codependent? Sure, yet devoted. The Alzheimers has blunted most of the hard edges in my father's personality. I purchased a pix and arranged with my pastor to bring Holy Communion to them as often as I could. Week after week, day by day, I watched my dear mother suffer, praying with her, just being with her, as her light grew dimmer.

Always faithful, William came with me to be with her many times. He had a knack for making my mother laugh. He told her he loved me, which consoled her. He prayed with her every time he visited. As for my father, ignoring my protests, William took advantage of the Alzheimers to announce to my father that he was planning to marry me.

"He loves finding out," William explained. My father "gave my hand" to him several times.

Contemplating life without my mother was deeply depressing.

"I'm not very good at suffering," my mother whispered to William one evening.

"Nobody is good at suffering," he replied, taking her hand. "In the Garden, even Jesus asked his Father to take it away from him."

Just days before she died, William calmly worked a miracle on Christmas night, relying on his lifelong devotion to Saint Anthony to find a priest to give her Last Rites when virtually every priest in the area was out of town or otherwise occupied with their own families for Christmas celebrations (which is understandable).

He spent hours on the phone, and we even drove to a nearby church named after Saint Anthony to feel spiritually closer to his saintly friend during our phone calls. Once there, we ran into two older ladies who had missed a prayer meeting. One stayed to make calls with us, and her helpful spirit distinctly reminded me of my mother.

None of us could get through. I was starting to lose hope. I understand that very few people care about or even know about Last Rites anymore, but I did not want my mother to pass away without experiencing this awesome final sacrament. Even William kept saying, "We need a miracle."

Then a priest heard about us through our newly-planted grapevine. When Father Michael finally arrived at the door, dressed in jeans because he had left a family gathering, I knew he was perfect for my mother: kind, patient, and soft-spoken. She was lucid and understood everything during her Last Rites (which is not required for this sublime sacrament to "work"). My father came over and knelt next to me and William, the three of us next to the kneeling priest. We all held hands.

Tears rolled down my face as I watched my mother receive the healing power of the anointing (which Father explained could heal the maladies of the soul and mind as well as the body), enjoyed complete absolution for her sins, and imbibed special graces to prepare her to traverse the "terrible doorway of death," as William calls it.

—◀◉

I was there when she died. Her passing was devastating. I wept for hours, day after day. I had difficulty getting anything done for my clients. For months into the new year I suffered the emotional pain of her loss.

It was impossible to know, of course, that cancer was growing inside me and was already taking its toll. I mistakenly attributed the loss of my typically bound-less energy solely to the mourning. The funeral did not seem to provide closure.

I missed my Mommy. Despite our strained relation-ship when I was young, we had spoken on the phone virtually every day for years. She was my best friend and now she was gone.

—◀◉

In recent days it was William who figured out what my insertion into the crucifixion scene at the Mission really meant. Jesus was preparing me for suffering. First, to suffer with my mother. Now, because of the cancer, physical and emotional suffering is with me all day, every day.

"This is your life now," Jesus told me.

There are brief interludes when I get an hour here or half a day there wherein I feel somewhat like a normal person. But mostly, I am in pain, usually for days at a time. I cannot remember the last time I slept through the night.

And what is the point of this book if I'm not honest with you? I become sad and depressed about this cancer and about possibly losing my future life with William. I snap at him sometimes because there is no one else to snap at. Thank God he ignores me—or laughs. He says I have an indefinite Free Pass "for cancer" and that I'm "not very good at being mean."

I have been trying my best to offer my suffering to Jesus, to be on the cross with Him. Father Bert tells me that my suffering helps God bring grace into the world for conversions and forgiveness in relationships when I give it to Christ.

Father says to "give" it to Jesus. William says to "climb up on the cross with Jesus because everybody there is His best friend."

I am so scared. Cancer is evil.

No one deserves this.

But Jesus was innocent, too.

When I was in the crucifixion scene at the Carmel Mission, I learned that part of the Blessed Mother's suffering was the injustice she felt because her son Jesus was innocent. Right now, around my neck, I am wearing my mother's Miraculous Medal which portrays Our Lady's heart with a sword running through it. When Mary and Joseph brought Jesus to the temple when he

was a baby, the old prophet Simeon predicted to her
that "your heart, too, a sword shall pierce, so that out
of many hearts thoughts will be revealed." A spiritual
sword went through her heart at the crucifixion.

Not long after we met, William gave me a three-inch
crucifix which contains a tiny piece of the True Cross
Jesus actually died on. It fits into my hand. I often hold
it when the pain "breaks through" the meds.

I squeeze it.

—◀◖◗

Billy called today. He's been devastated ever since finding out about my cancer and he promised he would do
anything to help me. We discussed private things—just
between us. I am so grateful to God he has broken the
cycle—both of us are miracles of grace, both of us are
hope for others. I really do forgive him and there will
always be a place in my heart for him.

—◀◖◗

It is becoming more difficult to dictate my story. I am
so, so very grateful for all my friends who come to visit,
whether I am recovering from the chemotherapy at my
apartment or when I was in the hospital.

My sister Theresa calls and I put her on speaker as
we chat like normal. I am also very close with her grown
children, Sarah and Adam, who text regularly. Sarah is
competing in the Miss America contest this summer so
I want to get better so I can be by her side like always.

It seems like hundreds of people are sending me cards
and flowers, contributing to the campaign to help pay
my mounting medical bills, and chiming in on social
media to support me. In addition to William, Jesus has
sent me a select few friends who are helping me cope,

caring for me, and staying with me in the hospital.

For years I worried I would be alone. Now God is sending so many selfless people to be with me.

Especially my true love, my William.

—◀◖◖

William prays with me every morning and every night. He brings me Holy Communion. We read the Gospel readings for the day and follow the prayers in a booklet for the sick. Then I receive the Sacred Host and talk to Jesus inside me. How did I go for weeks or months without the Eucharist when I was young?

Then we try to enjoy the day as much as we can. Because I live on the second floor, it took a long time today to go outside and stand in the grass in my bare feet. I had to hang on to my man for balance the whole time, but I managed. We tried to talk about when to get engaged, and where to settle down, but in our hearts…

Then I worked on this book.

William often tells me Jesus loves "His little girl." This makes me smile every time. I am a little girl. I talk to Jesus a lot now.

—◀◖◖

I decided to not shave off all my hair, even if some of it has fallen out. My hairstylist and colorist, Larina, one of my closest friends, did a wonderful job today making what remains look quite presentable, especially if I wear just the right kind of hat.

Style still matters to me, Girls.

William, who sports hair practically down to his shoulders (perfect for running my fingers through), crashed our session and asked Larina to give him a crewcut "out of solidarity." I know he did it to make me laugh. It worked, too.

I like it short on him.

—◄(◎

I am in the hospital again, this time being treated for a life-threatening blood clot (so dangerous the hospital's priest came to give me Last Rites again). I just heard terrible news. My father broke his hip and is now in the same hospital, two floors below me. He underwent surgery and it was considered a success but the staff tells me he refuses to eat—or that he may have forgotten *how to eat*. He pulls out the feeding tubes. He can be stubborn.

I cannot go to see him because of my own condition, but my brother's wife Dorie told me he is terribly sad. For months, because of his Alzheimers, during every hour of every day he has been "finding out" that his wife has died.

—◄(◎

I am home from the hospital, but can no longer care for myself. I have to have William, or dear Dorie, or one of my best friends with me all the time now. When Dorie prays over me and holds me, I feel the Spirit of God and can bear the pain better. Someone has to sleep on an air mattress in my room next to my bed every night, just in case.

Tonight it's Gigi's turn, although she has to leave in the morning. We grew up together and she survived pancreas replacement surgery many years ago. Sadly, because of her medical issues, she and her husband were not able to have children.

My father died today. I am so sad. *Daddy! Daddy!*
   I'm sorry—I cannot dictate this for you any longer.

Today I am feeling a little better physically even though I am heartbroken about my father. I might try to leave the apartment for social reasons for the first time since I was diagnosed. Gigi is driving back from her home four hours away to stay with me for several days and has promised to take me to a nearby shopping center tomorrow.

Gigi and I had a nice time shuffling slowly into a few stores. We picked out a lovely hat and I texted a photo of me wearing it to William. Physically, it was the best I have felt in two months. *Maybe the chemo is working,* I think. We'll know for sure when they do a scan in a few weeks.
   After purchasing the hat, we went to a department store. We turned a corner and suddenly we were in the baby section. I broke down into tears and so did Gigi. Surrounded by empty strollers and playpens, we held each other for a long time.

It's dark outside and I can't sleep. My true love has come into my room and is standing next to me at my bed. I am holding the True Cross he gave me so long ago, my eyes scrunched closed. I miss my Mommy and Daddy. So much pain. It never stops.

This is my life now.
I have to tell William something.
"I love this cross. I love this cross."

—✺—

Everything is worse. Pain is everywhere—in my back, my abdomen, my neck and legs. It feels like someone is running a sword through my shoulder where I had surgery several years ago.

It is very hard to breath sometimes.

Gigi, overwhelmed, had to call an ambulance service to take me to the emergency room when I had a seizure. William rushed here to be with me. The doctor ordered new scans to find out what's going on.

—✺—

The doctor came by this evening—very late, around 10:00 pm. My brother Tim and Dorie were here, along with William and Larina. My doctor is a good man with a kind voice and decades of experience.

The chemotherapy did not work. He stood at the foot of my bed and explained in medical terms why a cure is no longer possible. The doctor used the words "weeks" and "months."

Then Tim asked me, "Marianne, do you understand what the doctor is telling you?"

William was at my side, holding my hand, his face ashen from the lack of sleep, fatigue, and worry.

Did I understand? I held the gaze of my true love, ignoring everyone else.

"I'm going to die," I told him weakly.

William came to me this morning while I was sitting in a chair and told me in his direct way that he had been in the hospital chapel asking Jesus what to advise me in light of what the doctor told us last night. Between sobs he told me that my only job is to try to get to heaven as quickly as possible. He could barely get the words out.

"But I want to live," I told him.

He was sitting right in front of me. Close. Our faces were very close.

He looked at me, and I could see he was not peaceful or relaxed at all. Brokenhearted, like me.

"You know I love being with you, Baby Girl, every minute, even through all of this. I want you to live, too.

"But it's like I've been telling you—all your endings are happy endings. In heaven you're going to be outside of time, so it will only seem like an instant to you and then I will be there."

Then he repeated, kindly, firmly, "Marianne, let it take you. Your only job now is to get to heaven as fast as you can."

This is the man Jesus sent to me.

After my talk with William, my dear friend Rita—the one who introduced me to Father Bert—came in and we prayed a Rosary together. Larina texted me and she is coming in again tonight.

My beloved friend Elaine also came to visit me today. She started crying as soon as she sat down next to my bed. I asked her to help me sit up. Then, to help me stand. This took a while. After I was standing, I gave her a hug.

"Thank you for crying," I whispered to her. "It makes me feel loved." She began weeping again.

———❦———

I remember when Mary came to hug me after I cried out for a mother. I remember where I was with William on my birthday and the little girl with her mother on the beach and how happy we all were.

———❦———

I have decided to take my darling's advice. I hope there is an ocean there. When I get there I am going to go to the water with Angelica.

Epilogue

Love and Light

Marianne Collins passed away on the day after William spoke to her about heaven. She took her final labored breath in the early afternoon, surrounded by her siblings and their spouses, with her sister Roberta holding her right hand and William holding her left while he tenderly cupped the side of her face in his other hand.

Twelve hours earlier, during the early morning hours, Marianne had received Last Rites for the third time since her initial diagnosis seven weeks earlier. Not long after, addressing William, she made a great effort to whisper her final words on earth:

"I love you."

She lost consciousness.

He continued to converse with his true love through their guardian angels until the sun rose. After her room became bathed in a warm morning light, while glancing at her bed sheet, he read the word *Angelica* imprinted on it, five inches across in powder blue, repeated several times in a diamond grid. He began to weep tears beyond sorrow and joy.

A photograph of the sheet adorns the cover of this book. Later it was discovered this was a brand name for a specialized hospital linen manufacturer; neither he nor any of her other caretakers had seen a sheet bearing that name during any of Marianne's previous hospital stays.

—❧❀—

Father Bert's homily at Marianne's funeral focused on the significance of her example of offering her suffering to Christ Crucified for the salvation of souls and to help bring the grace of forgiveness into the world.

He also shared how he had exercised his authority to give Marianne an Apostolic Pardon during his administration of Last Rites to her, which spared her of any temporal punishment due to sin up to that point in her life. This means she would not likely spend any time in purgatory and would almost certainly immediately join Jesus, Our Lady, all the saints, the angels, and her daughter in everlasting life.

—❦⊙

William recited the following to conclude her eulogy:

Our Marianne
We cannot unhear her humming
We cannot untouch her hand
We can't unspin her
Or the galaxy's rings
As she dances
Oceans beneath her breast
Stars within her womb, waiting to be born.
You are always light
You are always love,
A little lamb
Our quiet dove.
You are always here
With your child king
Always, always, always,
Always smiling, always warm,
You are always always:
Christmas morn.

Asking for Marianne's Help

At the reception following the funeral Mass, her brother Tim placed a poster with the words "Love and Light," next to a podium. He explained that this was how Marianne always signed her emails and letters.

Dozens then came forward to publicly bear witness to her infectious joy, childlike nature, striking natural beauty, boundless vivaciousness, unfailing kindness, and, of course, her unique angelic light. It was clear she spent a great portion of her time on earth helping others; she was too humble to write in detail about the numerous charities for which she volunteered, including many dedicated to helping women and children.

The Catholic Church has long taught that our roles in heaven echo our good works on earth. Instantaneously after her death, those who knew her reported Marianne sending signs of consolation or answers to their prayers, usually accompanied by one of her two "calling cards." The first is a prominent display of the color pink. The other is a butterfly or an artistic image of one.

The publisher warmly invites you to ask Marianne, along with her namesakes, Immaculate Mary and her mother Saint Anne, to intercede to Jesus for you and your loved ones, especially if you or they have experienced abuse, are an abuser, have had or were involved with an abortion, or have unknowingly used abortifacient contraceptives or had relations with someone using them. If you need guidance, as she did, ask for help returning to the healing power of the Sacraments. She wants you to be close with Jesus, as she was. She wants you to enjoy the love of His mother, as she did. She wants you to enjoy God's Divine Mercy, as she did.

You can share how you were helped here:

www.catholicity.com/marianne

Marianne's Prayer
(from her journal on April 12, 2016)

Dear God, through this journal, the memories, and the torment, may I learn to forgive myself as Jesus has forgiven me. I am sorry Lord for all that I have done to hurt you, to hurt others, and to hurt myself. I humbly ask that you please continue to walk with me and guide me according to your will, not mine. Continue to create me to be the woman you want me to be. Use me for your good, dear Lord, so that I may be an instrument to help others through their time of suffering, trials, and triumphs. Thank you. Amen.

Saint Michael Prayer
(one of Marianne's favorites)
Saint Michael the Archangel, defend us in battle, be our defense against the wickedness and snares of the devil. May God rebuke him, we humbly pray, and do thou, O Prince of the heavenly host, by the power of God, cast into hell Satan and the other evil spirits who prowl about the world seeking the ruin of souls. Amen.

Marianne's Morning Prayer
Dear Lord, I do not know what will happen to me today—I only know that nothing will happen that was not foreseen by you and directed to my greater good from all eternity. I adore Your holy and unfathomable plans and submit to them with all my heart for love of you, the Pope, and the Immaculate Heart of Mary. Amen.

Would You Like to Introduce Marianne to Your...

Family

Friends

Social Networks

Prayer Group

Church or Parish

Business Associates

Local Bookstore Owner

Local School or Library

Pastor or Priest?

The Mary Foundation is here to help you. We will send you as many copies (dozens, hundreds, thousands) as you want for a nominal donation. Use the convenient form on the following pages or visit us online today:

www.catholicity.com

E-Book Editions Available
for a nominal donation on
Kindle, Apple and Google.

Suggested Resources

WEBSITES

Rachel's Vineyard Post-Abortion Healing (Counseling, Retreats)
rachelsvineyard.org

One More Soul (Reproductive Issues, Contraception)
onemoresoul.com

Human Life International (Reproductive Issues, Contraception)
hli.org

Janet Smith's Sexual Common Sense (Reproductive Issues, Contraception)
janetesmith.com

Theology of the Body (Human Sexuality)
theologyofthebody.net

Militia of the Immaculata (Consecration to Mary)
consecration.com

Catholic Answers (Catholicism and Faith)
catholic.com

TAN Books/Saint Benedict Press (Catholicism and Faith)
tanbooks.com

Lighthouse Catholic Media (Catholicism and Faith)
lighthousecatholicmedia.org

Catholics Come Home (Practical Guidance)
catholicscomehome.org

BOOKS

Forbidden Grief: The Unspoken Pain of Abortion (Healing)
Theresa Burke

33 Days to Morning Glory (Consecration to Mary)
Fr. Michael E. Gaitley, MIC

True Devotion to Mary (Mary Mother of God)
Saint Louis de Montfort

Rome Sweet Home (Protestant Minister Becomes Catholic)
Scott Hahn

FREE FROM THE MARY FOUNDATION
www.catholicity.com

CATHOLIC CDs

Bringing Catholics Home

Healing and Holiness

The Rosary and Divine Mercy Chaplet

The Conversion of Scott Hahn

Seven Secrets of the Eucharist

Confession

Knowing Jesus

The Eucharist Explained

Marian Apparitions Explained

BOOKLETS

Powerful Prayers Every Catholic Should Know

Going Back to Confession After Years or Decades

Seven Daily Habits of Faithful Catholics

NOVELS

Pierced by a Sword

Conceived Without Sin

House of Gold

How the Mary Foundation Works

- We will send up to ten free books. A donation is optional. Free shipping.

- Fast Delivery. All requests will be shipped on the day we receive your request.

- We will not give your personal information to other organizations.

- We only accept requests online or by mail. Outside the United States: only online orders will be accepted. www.catholicity.com

- We only send materials to those who write to us directly. Do not send us any address of people other than yourself.

- We welcome your feedback and opinions. Typographical and grammar suggestions are appreciated (include page and line number).

- Bookstores, retailers, groups, schools, and other organizations: please refer to our website for bulk discounts and promotional information.

Thank you for being a part of our work!

Order Your FREE Books

(Please Print)

Name: _____

Address: _____

City: _____

State: _____ Zip: _____

Email: _____
        For questions about your order and to receive the monthly CatholiCity email message.

Suggested **Optional** Donation for up to ten items: **$1 to $10 each.**
Minimum donation for **more than ten items: $1 to $5 each.**

Quantity: **Woman** by Marianne Collins (Books)   _____

                                X Donation per Book $ _____

                                = **Total Donation** $ _____

Optional Extra Gift for Shipping $ _____
Canada, Other Countries: You must order online using a credit card.
United States (Optional): Enter $10 for Fast Guaranteed Shipping.

Optional Extra Gift to Support Our Work $ _____

                        TOTAL DONATION $ _____

CatholiCity
FOR FASTEST DELIVERY
Order Online:
www.catholicity.com

Mary Foundation
Mail this Form to:
The Mary Foundation
PO Box 26101 • Fairview Park, OH 44126

Outside the U.S.: only online orders will be accepted. Make checks payable to "The Mary Foundation"
Your gift is tax deductible. We'll ship your materials the day we receive your letter or online order.
We only send materials to those who write us directly: don't send us any address other than your own.

How the Mary Foundation Works

- We will send up to ten free books. A donation is optional. Free shipping.

- Fast Delivery. All requests will be shipped on the day we receive your request.

- We will not give your personal information to other organizations.

- We only accept requests online or by mail. Outside the United States: only online orders will be accepted. www.catholicity.com

- We only send materials to those who write to us directly. Do not send us any address of people other than yourself.

- We welcome your feedback and opinions. Typographical and grammar suggestions are appreciated (include page and line number).

- Bookstores, retailers, groups, schools, and other organizations: please refer to our website for bulk discounts and promotional information.

Thank you for being a part of our work!

Order Your FREE Books

(Please Print)

Name: _____

Address: _____

City: _____

State: _____ Zip:_____

Email: _____
For questions about your order and to receive the monthly CatholiCity email message.

Suggested **Optional** Donation for up to ten items: **$1 to $10 each.**
Minimum donation for **more than ten items: $1 to $5 each.**

Quantity: **Woman** by Marianne Collins (Books)   _____

X Donation per Book $ _____

= Total Donation $ _____

Optional Extra Gift for Shipping $ _____
Canada, Other Countries: You must order online using a credit card.
United States (Optional): Enter $10 for Fast Guaranteed Shipping.

Optional Extra Gift to Support Our Work $ _____

TOTAL DONATION $ _____

CatholiCity.
FOR FASTEST DELIVERY
Order Online:
www.catholicity.com

Mary Foundation.
Mail this Form to:
The Mary Foundation
PO Box 26101 • Fairview Park, OH 44126

Outside the U.S.: only online orders will be accepted. Make checks payable to "The Mary Foundation"
Your gift is tax deductible. We'll ship your materials the day we receive your letter or online order.
We only send materials to those who write us directly: don't send us any address other than your own.

How the Mary Foundation Works

- We will send up to ten free books. A donation is optional. Free shipping.

- Fast Delivery. All requests will be shipped on the day we receive your request.

- We will not give your personal information to other organizations.

- We only accept requests online or by mail. Outside the United States: only online orders will be accepted. www.catholicity.com

- We only send materials to those who write to us directly. Do not send us any address of people other than yourself.

- We welcome your feedback and opinions. Typographical and grammar suggestions are appreciated (include page and line number).

- Bookstores, retailers, groups, schools, and other organizations: please refer to our website for bulk discounts and promotional information.

Thank you for being a part of our work!

— Order Your FREE Books —

(Please Print)

Name:_____

Address:_____

City: _____

State: _____ Zip:_____

Email: _____
      For questions about your order and to receive the monthly CatholiCity email message.

Suggested **Optional** Donation for up to ten items: **$1 to $10 each.**
Minimum donation for **more than ten items: $1 to $5 each.**

Quantity: **Woman** by Marianne Collins (Books)   _____

X Donation per Book **$** _____

= Total Donation $ _____

Optional Extra Gift for Shipping $ _____
Canada, Other Countries: You must order online using a credit card.
United States (Optional): Enter $10 for Fast Guaranteed Shipping.

Optional Extra Gift to Support Our Work $ _____

TOTAL DONATION $ _____

Catholi**City**.
FOR FASTEST DELIVERY
Order Online:
www.catholicity.com

Mary Foundation.
Mail this Form to:
The Mary Foundation
PO Box 26101 • Fairview Park, OH 44126

Outside the U.S.: only online orders will be accepted. Make checks payable to "The Mary Foundation"
Your gift is tax deductible. We'll ship your materials the day we receive your letter or online order.
We only send materials to those who write us directly: don't send us any address other than your own.